WHITE CANYON

**Remembering the little Town
At the Bottom of Lake Powell**

By

Tom McCourt

Second Edition
Revised and Updated

ISBN-13: 978-0-9741568-6-6
Library of Congress Control Number: 2018908410

Published by Southpaw Publications ☙
Printed by Press Media, Provo, Utah
Cover design by Tom Mc Court

About the Cover Photo

The cover photo was taken in 1952 in front of the boardinghouse in the little town of White Canyon. The woman is the author's grandmother, Bertha Winn. The little girl is a cousin, Janis Winn York. The "boardinghouse" was a rough-cut-board and tarpaper dining hall that served as the business and social center of the town. In those years shortly after the second world war, the company-sponsored, transient and field expedient town had a military look and feel about it. Note the sign above the door that says Mess Hall.

Misty sunrise over the Bears Ears
Author photo

White Canyon

To Lorin and Bertha Winn
I'll meet you in White Canyon at the end of the trail.

Contents

Preface to the 2003 First Edition

Before we start, it should be understood that White Canyon is three things to me: a town, a canyon, and a state of mind. White Canyon Town was founded in 1949. White Canyon Wash stretches forty-five miles from Elk Ridge to Lake Powell on the east side of Glen Canyon, and that's where the name of the town came from. But when I speak of White Canyon in this book, I am sometimes referring to a five-mile section of the Colorado River Canyon, for that is how I understood the term when I was a boy.

White Canyon was where my grandparents lived, and after the town was gone they stayed for two more years. We still went to White Canyon to see them. To me, White Canyon has always been the very upper end of Glen Canyon, from the confluence of the Dirty Devil River to the mouth of White Canyon Wash. Today we can stand on the Hite Overlook on Highway 95 and look down on the flooded river valley that was the White Canyon of my childhood.

Preface to the 2018 Second Edition

It has been fifteen years since I wrote this little book. I have learned a lot in those years. Since this book was first printed I have been contacted by several people who knew and loved White Canyon. Some have sent me photographs and shared personal stories about their time spent in that little town and the surrounding canyon county. I have also corresponded with scholars of Utah and San Juan County history who have further enlightened me about certain events and people of note from the history of Glen Canyon.

Two important updates in this second edition are: I now know my grandfather was wrong about the location of Cass Hite's Dandy Crossing. And, the mystery of the Spanish writing in North Wash has been solved. Details are in the text.

Also, water levels in Lake Powell have dropped more than 100 feet since the late 1990s and the desert has reclaimed much of the original shore line. Twenty-first century low water levels now reveal some of the things that were submerged in the 1960s that were never expected to be seen again. The author and his wife have had some remarkable adventures exploring what the late University of Utah professor, C. Gregory Crampton, called, "The Ghosts of Glen Canyon." Details are in the text.

Acknowledgments

The skeleton of this work comes from the memories of a little boy. It is through the good graces of my aunts and uncles that I have been able to give it flesh and substance. Jack and Melba Winn have been invaluable to me, as have Nathan and Lorraine Noyes.

I have asked them to recall specific events, and to describe in detail trivial things like tablecloths, road signs and shingles. They in turn have been wonderful. They have given me pictures, documents, old letters and newspaper clippings. They were good to call me on the phone when some small gem of useful information finally came into focus. Lucky for me, I have tolerant relatives and I'm sure it has been a labor of love for all of us.

My Cousin, Janis Winn York, has been a big help. She remembers White Canyon through the eyes of a little girl and she tells the story with stars in her eyes, and sometimes tears. She knew my Grandmother's heart like no one else.

My brother Reed has been the backup file to my own memories. It is to him I have often gone to ask, "Do you remember the time …?" Reed stood by my side through this whole adventure, and when I describe something in this book, know that he experienced it with me. Reed has always been my best friend as well as my brother. This little book is a reflection of his heart, mind and memories, too.

Thank you to former White Canyon Town dwellers, Dan Marsing and Jeanie Foster McDoniel, who, after reading the first edition of this book, shared with me many photographs and memories of their time spent in that special corner of southeast Utah. Several of their photographs are included in this second edition. Thank you to historian and author James Knipmeyer, who solved the riddle of the Spanish writings in North Wash and set me straight about the location of Dandy Crossing.

Then, I owe a special thank you to Maurine Dorman who graciously poured through her late husband's files and records to search for photos and documents of White Canyon and the Southern Cross Uranium Company. She gave me treasures more precious than gold that will be handed down in my family for generations to come.

And finally, a big hug and a kiss to my pretty wife Jeannie, my companion, conscience and editor of first resort. She is the one who would invariably hand back a first draft and smugly tell me to do it again; "I can't smell the campfire yet." At her feet I lay the blame for any excesses of exuberant verbosity (wink).

Introduction

The little town of White Canyon was born a child of the uranium boom of the late 1940s. She was a special child and a sign in the heavens heralded her birth - that first atomic flash that lit the night sky over Alamogordo, New Mexico in July 1945.

A man named Arthur (Arth) Chaffin unknowingly chose her birthplace in 1946 when he constructed a homemade ferryboat that made it possible to move trucks and heavy equipment across the Colorado River at Hite. The town was born in 1949 when construction began on a uranium processing mill at the mouth of White Canyon, to process ore from the nearby Happy Jack Mine.

The town flourished for five years, but in 1954 the mill was closed and the town died. The waters of Lake Powell covered her remains ten years later. As the scars of her foundations slipped beneath the waves, all traces of her existence were lost. Her name was purged from our road signs, maps and memories and she disappeared from the consciousness of the nation. Most people who frequent the area today don't know she ever lived.

A few of us remember White Canyon. It was a special place to my family and me. In many ways that river canyon was the cradle that nurtured my mother's family into adulthood. It was there where my uncles took young wives and babies to start new lives together. It was there where uncles and aunts found their first real jobs and grown-up responsibilities. It was there where my maternal grandparents lived what were probably the best and happiest years of their lives. It was there where I first became truly aware of my surroundings and the promise of my life.

Brother Reed and I, along with cousins Janis, Lauren, Jill and Winn were nurtured there in love and happiness by that extended family group. I always knew I was someone special because I had a place among such people. I always felt wanted and loved, and I basked in the warmth of that feeling while surrounded by the most beautiful country in the world. It was truly wonderful. Every child should have such a beginning.

Like all good travelers, I see more than I remember and remember more than I see.
Benjamin Disraeli, British Prime Minister, 1870s.

Lake Powell at the confluence of White Canyon and Glen Canyon near Hite. Orientation is west. Henry Mountains in the distant background. White Canyon enters the lake at left center of the photograph. The town of White Canyon was in the right center of the photograph beneath the white arrow and 200 feet below the surface of the lake.

Author photo

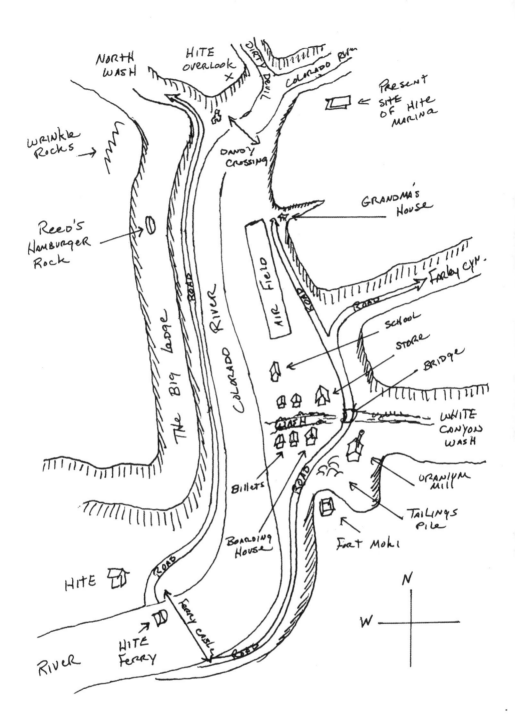

White Canyon Town and Valley
Scale inexact – approximately five miles top to bottom
The site marked Dandy Crossing is incorrect, as explained in the text

1
In the Beginning

Most people think the Garden of Eden was green and well watered, but some of us know it was red rock and sand. The Garden of Eden was a rock garden, a beautiful, sculpted rock garden. God loved the place and He molded the soft sandstone in the image of His home in the heavens.

For countless eons of time the Colorado River chewed down through the sandstone while the wind polished the sharp edges smooth. The sun baked the soft stone with warmth and glazed it with desert varnish. Sagebrush, bunchgrass, wild flowers and cacti fulfilled the full measure of their creation, adding color, texture and variety to the canyon country. Cottonwood and Juniper trees dug deep in the warm sand and their roots grew strong. Raptors and ravens winged high overhead and rejoiced in the majesty of it all.

The canyons were quiet but for the songs of the elements, the whisper of wind, a far-off rumble of thunder, the tinkle of moving water and the rustle of cottonwood leaves. The garden remained empty and waiting for a long, long time.

Then the people came. Only a few to begin with, but others soon followed. They were ice-age hunters who trekked into the canyons with flint-tipped spears, following the tracks of Pleistocene bison, ground sloth, and mammoth. The canyons welcomed them and sheltered them from the cold winds.

In the centuries that followed, as the ice retreated far to the north, some of the people stayed in the warm and friendly canyons. The large mammals disappeared but the canyon people learned to hunt smaller game, deer, mountain sheep, rabbits and antelope. They also made seasonal migrations through Mother Nature's open-air pantries gathering fruits, nuts and seeds. Archaeologists call that lingering remnant of the ice age hunters the Desert Archaic Culture.

The early people left few reminders of their passing. They lived within the bounds of the natural world and reconciled themselves to what it offered them. Here and there they stained the roof of an overhanging ledge with smoke from cooking fires or left scattered chips of flint among the sand dunes. But they remain a mysterious people, long faded into the sands and the years.

And yet, the Desert Archaic peoples left us a glimpse into their very souls. In a few hidden places they left the imprints of their hands, hearts and minds on the sandstone walls of the canyons. The paintings they made reach out with power and span the centuries, reflecting a sense of artistry, symmetry and style that belies the notion that the early canyon dwellers were crude and brutish cavemen.

Many of the paintings depict "ghost figures," surreal humanoid beings lacking arms and legs and with huge haunting eyes. Do they represent gods, ghouls, extraterrestrials, mythical creatures, peyote-induced illusions or the spirits of ancestors? The question has been debated since the mid-1800s.

Barrier Canyon pictograph near Thompson Springs, north of Moab, Utah
Author photo

Ancient paintings of this type are called Barrier Canyon style, named after the location where they were first documented and studied. Barrier Canyon pictographs[1] are found only in southeast Utah, and the magnificent site that gave them that name is located in a westerly extension of Canyonlands National Park that is now called Horseshoe Canyon.

In the Beginning

Barrier Canyon paintings are generally found on the west side of the Colorado River, from the Book Cliffs on the north, to the Henry Mountains on the south. They extend west of the river across the San Rafael Swell and Castle Valley to the Wasatch mountains.

The descendants of the ancient artists became the Basketmakers. Their children had history, traditions and roots in the canyon country. Those grandchildren of the ice age hunters still hunted and gathered for their livelihood, but they were becoming more settled. They were learning to plant corn and they made snug little dens in the dirt. Their dens would be called pit houses by later peoples.

Pit houses were shallow, roundish depressions dug down in the ground with a covering of poles, willows and brush, plastered with clay. They were like little beaver houses, small, tight and warm. The people were still artists, but their art took a different form. They wove beautiful baskets, sandals and belts from the native plants and grasses.

Over the centuries, the children of the Basketmakers went even farther and learned to make beautiful pottery and houses of stone. They became full-time farmers and skilled agricultural technicians who tamed the harsh environment and bent it to serve their will. We sometimes call them Anasazi, a Navajo word suggesting, "Ancient Ones." [2]

There were thousands of Ancient Ones, and their monuments are everywhere in the canyon country. Southern Utah is dotted with little cliff houses and low mounds of fire-blackened earth. The canyons produced food abundantly for them and their children were healthy and strong.

The Anasazi settled in tiny villages and far-flung family farmsteads out on the mesa tops. God sent them rain and they dry-farmed much of the canyon country, something that can't be done today. They had an intricate network of trails, little sandal-beaten byways that connected the farms, villages and sacred places. Broken shards of painted pottery still mark their pathways through the desert like the breadcrumb trails of Hansel and Gretel.

They learned to utilize every drop of water in the beautiful but harsh environment. Little stone dikes and small rainwater catch-basins can still be found in many small washes and desert canyons. They terraced sloping canyon rims and ditched rain water to little backyard-sized gardens. They grew healthy crops and waxed fat for a while.

Then, mysteriously, they began to build forts and lookout towers. A dark shadow of fear crept over the landscape. The people abandoned family farms and retreated into larger and larger villages where there was safety in numbers. Eventually they moved their towns into sheltering caves that were more easily defended. [3]

And suddenly, they were gone. The rock houses, granaries, irrigation dikes and watch towers all fell into ruin and decay. The land was vacant and silent again. Rain fell on unplanted fields and the wind moaned through the empty ruins.

The canyons remained empty and quiet for a long time. The fields of the Anasazi became overgrown with brush and grass. Coyotes denned among the ruins and ravens nested on watchtower walls. Occasionally a Ute, Paiute, or Navajo would wander through the area hunting and gathering, but there is little evidence that any of them called Glen Canyon home.

In 1776, five hundred years after the Anasazi disappeared, a Spanish priest, Fray Francisco Silvestre Escalante, and a band of bold explorers touched the fringes of the canyon country. Undoubtedly there had been other Spaniards there before them, but there are few records. Escalante came with the sanction of the church and the Spanish governor, so his travels were recorded. Others were not so eager to have their wanderings known. Private exploration was illegal in early Spanish America.

Mysteriously, between Abiquiu, New Mexico and the Dolores River of Western Colorado near Nucla, Escalante found the country empty. There were ancient ruins and shards of broken pottery scattered in the canyons, but no man or habitation was found in three hundred miles of wilderness travel.

On the return journey, Escalante and his party plumbed the depths of Glen Canyon and crossed the Colorado at a place known ever after as the Crossing of the Fathers. They were probably not the first Europeans to cross Glen Canyon, but they were the first to leave a sure record.

As the little caravan of the Padres faded into the heat shimmer of the Arizona desert, Glen Canyon fell silent again and remained that way for another lifetime. Then, Jacob Hamblin, an early Mormon missionary to the Indians, and his small party of explorers, followed Escalante's faded footprints through the Crossing of the Fathers in 1858. They made only a small splash as they crossed the river and continued on their way. They made no effort to settle or fully explore the rugged canyon country. They were on their way to Oraibi, then back to Kanab and St. George, Utah.

Then, in 1869, and again in 1872, a one-armed civil war veteran named John Wesley Powell came bobbing down the river in a little wooden boat. Major Powell was an incredible man. He had given his right arm to the Union cause at the battle of Shiloh during the American Civil War. Yet he had the courage and tenacity to face the depths and perils of the unknown canyons of the Colorado with his empty shirtsleeve pinned to his side. A man tempered by many trials, he was strong, brave, thoughtful and perceptive. Major Powell and his companions stopped to visit a magnificent Indian ruin at the mouth of White Canyon and they made some sketches.[4]

Major Powell would bring the canyon country to the attention of the world. He found Glen Canyon to be truly spectacular, and in 1873 he went home to write about his adventures, give lectures and revel in his conquest. The canyons would lay empty and quiet again for a few more years.

Notes:

1. Pictographs are painted on the rocks. Petroglyphs are carved into the rock.

2. It has become widely accepted in recent years to call the ancient peoples of the four-corners area "Ancestral Puebloans." But the author is a Geezer from the old school and the Anasazi have been his friends for many years. He's not sure he knows the Ancestral Puebloans.

3. Steven A. LeBlanc. *Prehistoric Warfare in the American Southwest*. University of Utah Press. 1999.

4. Later prospectors and pioneers named this ruin Fort Moki. It plays a major role in this narrative.

RUINS ON THE BRINK OF GLEN CANYON.

John Wesley Powell expedition sketch of the Indian ruin at the mouth of White Canyon. Later explorers and prospectors would name the ruin Fort Moki. The term Moki, or Moqui, was used in the 1800s to denote all Pueblo Indians, current and ancient.

2
The Hole in the Rock Expedition

No history of Glen Canyon can be properly told without including the story of The Hole in the Rock Expedition. This incredible adventure was lived by faithful Mormons from southwest Utah who had been called by church leaders to claim and settle the San Juan River valley. To get to the San Juan river valley they had to cross Glen Canyon, and no one had ever done that with wagons.

It was the "manifest destiny" of the American people, and a religious obligation for early Mormon converts, to beat back the wilderness and make it a place of peaceful habitation. It was a sacred duty to purge the wilderness of the "wasters and destroyers," in the words of Brigham Young. The wasters and destroyers were all forms of predators, wolves, coyotes, cougars, bears, eagles and untamed and uncouth men. Renegade white men were to be brought to the bar of justice or driven from the territory. Indians were to be taught the arts of civilization and rescued from their supposed brutishness. Indians were to be treated "kindly," but since they were not making proper civilized use of the land, they could be pushed aside and hopefully brought back into the fold later when their children might be more enlightened and agreeable. This was the mindset of nineteenth century America.

For a Mormon family to be "called" to settle a wilderness area was to be given a holy mission to conquer the land and make it "blossom as the rose" (Isaiah 35:1). God had given man dominion over the land and all of God's lesser creatures. It was man's duty to make it a garden again. A man was serving God and his fellow man when he staked a claim in a wilderness area and carved out a prosperous farm through toil, sweat and personal sacrifice. He was preparing the land for those who would follow - his children and his grandchildren. He was creating a place for his descendants to live in peace and prosperity. He was building a Kingdom of God on earth. Wilderness, wildness, predatory beasts, uncivilized men and unconquered nature were impediments to the Kingdom of God.

An exploring party was sent out in April 1879 to select a route for the San Juan pioneers. Very little was known of the San Juan river basin and there were no roads into the country. The exploring party set out from Paragonah, Utah and crossed the Colorado River at Lee's Ferry at the top of Grand Canyon. They then went deep into Arizona. In Arizona they turned north across the Navajo lands to find the San Juan River.

White Canyon

After locating a reasonably good place for a settlement, a place they called "Montezuma," the scouts returned to central Utah by way of The Old Spanish Trail. The full journey of the exploring party was a thousand-mile circle. And because of the distance and the hostility of the Navajos, the southern route through Arizona was deemed to be impractical. The explorers recommended that the settlers take The Old Spanish Trail on their colonizing mission back to the valley of the San Juan. The Old Spanish Trail was a well established route, and by going that way, their journey would be about 400 miles. The trip would probably take between six and eight weeks.

But, the impatient settlers were anxious to begin work on their new farms before planting season and they didn't want to spend any unnecessary time with travel. Instead of taking good and reasonable advice, they resolved instead to gather at the frontier town of Escalante and trust God to show them a more direct route across the unexplored canyons. They had no idea what they were asking of God, or of themselves.

During the early winter of 1879, the expedition left Escalante and traveled to the rim of Glen Canyon. There were about 230 people, 83 wagons and a herd of livestock estimated to be 1000 head. They started out with high hopes and great expectations, believing the journey to the San Juan would only take a few weeks. They didn't know it yet, but their unexplored "shortcut" would take them on a backbreaking odyssey that would last for six months.

When they reached the western rim of Glen Canyon they found themselves stopped by the huge vertical walls of the massive river canyon. They could find no way to get down from the canyon rim. The river lay at their feet, almost two thousand feet below. Desperately they searched for a way to get to the river, but only sheer walls and impossible tributary canyons were available.

Finally they found a crack, a "hole in the rock" that a skinny goat couldn't squeeze through, and they began to chisel and dynamite a wagon road down. They lowered workers over the ledge in barrels to drill, with hammer and steel, holes into the rock for the blasting powder. They shoveled tons of sand into the crevice to fill holes between big rocks, and they made a near-vertical wagon trail down to the river.

The "road" was a 25% grade overall, and as steep as 45% in some places. Along one stretch where the road passed close against a towering rock wall, they had to drill holes in the ledge and pound oak stakes in the holes. They then "bridged over" the stakes with poles and brush to widen the road. On the near-vertical sandstone side they cut a groove into the rock with axes and chisels for the wagon wheels to follow. It took more than a month and a half to cut the quarter-mile of road down through the sandstone.

When the road was finally ready for the hazardous descent, wagon wheels were rough-locked with logs and chains and several men followed each wagon down trying to hold it back with ropes as it slid down the chute. On every descent, a man had to sit high on the wagon seat to try to steer the team of horses as the wagon pushed them down the slot. Water barrels on the sides of wagons were smashed against the rock walls and the lurching wagons sometimes jerked the men following with ropes off their feet and dragged them down the roadbed. Women and children walking down the grade reported that in some places the rocks became so slick from iron horseshoes and iron-rimmed wagon wheels the people had to slide down parts of the slope on their backsides. The rocks were polished smooth and people wearing leather shoes could not keep their footing.

God must have been traveling with them, for it is truly incredible that no one was killed or seriously injured as the wagons slid, teetered and bumped down that near-vertical slide.

At the river they crossed the wagons on a raft and swam the animals across. They then scratched and clawed their way up and out of the canyon on the east side. It was a Herculaneum effort that drained them of strength, resources and valuable time.

Ironically, within a year, a much better river crossing was found about 35 miles upstream near the mouth of Hall's creek. It became known as Hall's crossing. Charles Hall from Escalante discovered the place and ran a ferry there for about five years during the 1880s. Today, on the east side of the canyon is Halls Crossing Marina, serving tourists on Lake Powell.

After crossing the river, the pioneers pulled, pushed and prayed their wagons over slickrock ridges, sand dunes, Grey Mesa, and the Clay Hill Divide. They finally staggered into the headwaters of White Canyon at a place they called Harmony Flat at the base of Elk Ridge. It had taken them six weeks to travel the fifty miles between the river crossing and Harmony flat. They had to shovel a road and double-team wagons most of the way. Their heroic best efforts had bought them an average of a mile a day.

In March 1880 they rested at Harmony Flat for a few days. The scenic wonder that was to become Natural Bridges National Monument was just a short distance to the northwest, but there is no mention they ever saw it. They were much too tired to do unnecessary exploring. They had been on the trail for most of five months and they were still a long way from their destination.

White Canyon

After resting those few days at Harmony Flat, the pioneers resumed their ordeal toward the east. They soon became entangled in a "cedar forest" and had to send men ahead with axes to cut a trail through the juniper trees. Breaking through Cedar Mesa, they bumped into Comb Ridge and were forced to skirt that impenetrable barrier to the south. Scouts found an ancient Indian trail through Comb Ridge (highway 95 follows that trail today) but it was a footpath and they couldn't get wagons through. Instead they cut a trail down Road Canyon to the foot of the comb, and then followed Comb Wash to the San Juan River. When they got to the river, they found they were boxed in. They couldn't follow the river upstream, and they couldn't cross the river either.

They were given one last torture to bear in the form of a slickrock trail they called the San Juan Hill (eighteen years before Teddy Roosevelt and Cuba). There was no other way around. San Juan Hill was so steep they had to use seven spans of horses (14 horses), to pull each wagon up the near-vertical slickrock trail. It is said the trail was painted with blood from the skinned knees and legs of the struggling horses, and many years later, normally stoic old men wept when telling the tale.

They finally reached the San Juan River Basin in April 1880 and dropped from exhaustion some eighteen miles short of their intended destination. Men and animals were just too tired to travel those few remaining miles to their pre-selected site at the mouth of Montezuma Creek. And, their horses were in such bad shape from exhaustion, crippling bruises, cuts and contusions, they just couldn't ask any more of them. The Mormons made camp where they fell and christened the place Bluff City in honor of the stark river bluffs that looked down on their homesteading efforts. Today's little town of Bluff, Utah is the fruit of that heroic pioneering effort.

In one of those wicked little twists of fate, the settlers soon found there was not enough farmland along the river for all of them to make a living. Some had to go back to the Mormon settlements in western Utah and try to find a new home elsewhere.

Notes:

Read David E. Miller. *Hole In The Rock.* University of Utah Press. 1966.

A replica of the old pioneer town and some of the original log cabins and furnishings have been preserved as a historic landmark. It is called the Bluff Fort Historic Site and Visitor Center, and is well worth seeing when visiting southeast Utah.

Young tourists at the Bluff Fort Historic Site in Bluff, Utah
Author photo

White Canyon

Wagon road through the Hole in the Rock
Lake Powell in the background
Author photo

3
Cass Hite

Cass Hite was the man who first brought "civilization" to upper Glen Canyon. A pioneer, explorer, prospector and entrepreneur, pretentious enough to call his lonely little cabin on the desert, "Hite City." Cass was the first non-Indian to settle the area, and his legend, legacy and name are important parts of the history of Glen Canyon.

Cass Hite 1890
Hosteen-Pish-La-Ki was his Navajo name
which is interpreted as, "Mister Silver."

Little is known of Cass Hite's early life. He was rumored to be a civil war veteran, a confederate rebel who fought with Quantrill's Raiders in Missouri and Kansas. The rumor has never been verified and is probably not true. Quantrill's Raiders was an unconventional guerrilla outfit of two or three hundred men. They fought as guerrilla soldiers, hit and run, hide, then reappear unexpectedly. The Union Army branded them as outlaws. The group produced such notables as Frank and Jesse James and Cole Younger, famous thieves and murderers in the 1870s. The largest battle they ever fought was the sacking of the little town of Lawrence Kansas in 1863. There they murdered almost 200 civilians while looting and burning the town. As a consequence they were hunted by Abe Lincoln's troops and shot down like predatory animals. The leader of the outfit, twenty-seven year old Captain William Quantrill, was killed in a Union ambush in 1865. By then the war was already lost, and the group, leaderless and facing a hangman's noose, disbanded and scattered to the winds without a formal surrender.

While there is no evidence Cass was ever a member of that unholy band of marauders, he was the type of man who would have encouraged the rumor. The story fit his inflated self-image and earned him some cautious respect as a man not to be messed with.

Cass Hite wandered onto the pages of history when he showed up along the San Juan River in 1880. He was there to investigate rumors of a lost Navajo silver mine. In January 1880, Indians in Monument Valley had killed two prospectors, James Merrick and Ernest Mitchell. When a search party found the bodies, the men had lumps of high-grade silver ore in their pockets. This was the stuff of legends, and prospectors searched Monument Valley into the twentieth century looking for the lost Merrick and Mitchell Silver Mine. No silver has ever been found there.

It took a lot of nerve in those days for a white man to venture into the Navajo country on the Utah-Arizona border, but Cass Hite was up to the challenge. He not only kept his scalp, but actually made friends with the Navajos. He found no secret silver mines, but somehow managed to befriend the legendary Navajo Chief, Hoskinnini.

Hoskinnini was one of the old-time Navajos who fought Kit Carson and the U.S. Army in the early 1860s. At the time, the Navajos were causing trouble and raiding white settlements in Utah, New Mexico and Arizona. In 1862 General James Carleton sent the aging (54 years old) but still famous frontiersman and scout, Kit Carson, to lead 700 troops into the Navajo heartland to teach the rascals a lesson. Colonel Kit Carson was brutal, and he got the job done.

Hoskinnini was one of the few Navajos to evade capture during the Navajo war. About 300 Navajos were killed, another 8500 imprisoned and taken on "The long walk" to Fort Sumner, New Mexico. Hoskinnini and his little band of about twenty renegades (men, women and children) hid out in the vastness of the canyons until their friends and families were released from federal custody in 1868.

Hoskinnini was a man steeled by starvation, deprivation and sore trials. The American army had scattered his family, killed his sheep and horses, burned his home and cut down his peach trees. His Navajo name, Hush-Kaaney (anglicized as Hoskinnini) is said to mean "The angry one." After 1868, The Angry One and his Navajo soldiers patrolled Monument Valley and did their very best to keep the white men out. The government had given them Monument Valley by treaty and Hoskinnini intended to keep it as a Navajo homeland.

Hoskininni Rock on the rim of White Canyon
Author photo

Into this environment Cass Hite entered Monument Valley, searching for the lost silver mine. The full details of his adventures among the Indians have been lost to history, but Cass told people in later years that it was his friend Hoskinnini who told him there was gold on the Colorado. Just how he pulled it off we will never know, but he may have scored some points by telling Hoskinnini the lie about how he too had fought the U.S. Army as a Confederate soldier and never surrendered.

White Canyon

Cass Hite built a log cabin of driftwood logs gleaned from along the riverbank. He planted a garden and explored the canyon country for miles around. He also spent many long days panning for gold on the sand and gravel bars near his new wilderness home.

Hite found a little gold, and when he took his yellow dust to town he started the Glen Canyon gold rush. Thousands of lusty prospectors pounded the old Indian trails into the canyon country to fill their pockets with riches. There was a mad scramble all up and down the river. Men staked claims on the gravel bars and mud flats. They panned and set up sluice boxes and scoured the sandstone ridges for that elusive vein of quartz. Some gold was found, but it was a fine powder and not the fat, lumpy nuggets of California. Colorado River gold was very difficult to recover, and in the end, more gold was poured into the canyons than taken out of them. The Glen Canyon gold rush waxed and waned by degrees, from the late 1880s through the second decade of the twentieth century.

Cass Hite made a little money panning for gold, and he had the good sense to capitalize on the gold rush he had started. He sold a lot of questionable mining claims, and he opened a store in his log cabin along the river. Then, in 1889 the government established a post office at his cabin to serve the miners in the canyon. Hite City was truly born at last. It became the hub of all mining activity in the Glen Canyon area. Mail and supplies for the store were packed in on horseback from the railroad town of Green River, over 100 miles away.

Cass Hite explored the river canyons extensively. He found a good spot for a second cabin in Ticaboo Canyon, about fifteen miles downstream from Hite. He told people Ticaboo was an Indian word that means "friend" or "friendly." There was a gravel bar at the mouth of Ticaboo Cass called, The Bank Of Ticaboo. He staked a mining claim there. He told people that all the gold he would ever need was there in the sand and gravel. When he needed money he simply took his gold pan and made a withdrawal. He said it was easier for him to safeguard his treasure by keeping it in the dirt and away from greedy bankers and other outlaws.

Cass Hite is credited with discovering the natural bridges at the head of White Canyon. Those same natural bridges Hoskinnini had shown him. Teddy Roosevelt made the site Utah's first national monument in 1908 after the National Geographic Society published an article about the sandstone wonders. Cass is also credited with discovering and naming the Dandy Crossing of the Colorado River.

The Colorado was a formidable barrier to wilderness travel in those days, and Hite's Dandy Crossing was the best place to cross the river in more than 300 miles. It was the only good place to cross the river between the Old Spanish Trail crossing near Moab, and Lee's Ferry at the top of Grand Canyon.

Hite City 1898
Used by permission, Utah State Historical Society

There were a few other crossing points, but they were poor second choices. The break-your-neck Hole In The Rock crossing was the better part of 100 miles downstream from Dandy Crossing, and incredibly, people from Bluff City used it for a year with wagon traffic going both ways. Halls crossing and ferry were about fifty miles south of Hite, but the roads to and from the site were an adventure. It was abandoned in the mid-1880s. The Crossing of the Fathers was a few miles upstream from Lee's Ferry, but the Escalante party had to cut steps in the slickrock to get their mules to the river. No wagon ever crossed the river there.

Cass Hite proudly accepted credit for discovering the Dandy Crossing, but it was undoubtedly his Indian friends who showed the place to him. The

Indians had used the crossing for millennia, and there is some evidence that early Spanish explorers might have crossed the river there as well.[1]

While it was a good place to cross the river, the Dandy Crossing was not a ford. It was too deep to ever wade across. Animals had to swim and people made use of boats or rafts. The charm of the place was that it offered easy approaches on either side of the river. People could cross the river there and continue on their way following smooth and near-level ground, which was a rare thing for the canyons of the Colorado. On the east side, a good trail followed White Canyon toward the Elk Ridge country and the Bears Ears toward Blanding. On the west side of the river, at Hite, a traveler could follow an old wagon road up Trachyte Creek or go through North Wash to Hanksville.

For years many people have believed that Cass Hite ran a ferryboat at Dandy Crossing. Evidence suggests he did not. He probably helped people cross the river, and he may have kept a boat there, or a raft, but there was no official Hite Ferry until the mid-1940s, in spite of what Cass Hite sometimes told the newspapers.

Notes:

1. Hoskinanni showed Cass Hite where early Spanish explorers had panned for gold along the river near where Cass built his cabin. And, Spanish inscriptions have been found a few miles up the river at a place called Spanish Bottoms.

Two books have been written about Cass Hite since this book was first published in 2003: A historical novel by Tom McCourt. *King of the Colorado: The Story of Cass Hite, Utah's Legendary Explorer, Prospector and Pioneer.* Southpaw Publications. 2012. And, A biography by James Knipmeyer. *Cass Hite: The Life of an Old Prospector.* University of Utah Press. 2016.

Cass Hite

Cass Hite's Dandy Crossing of the Colorado River - 1955

This is essentially the same view covered by the map on pageon page xv. The Chaffin (Hite) ferry is in the river at lower left. Note the sandbars in the middle of the river. Hite was on the left (west) bank of the river. White Canyon Town on the right (east) bank. The town was gone when this picture was taken. The white spot in upper right is the mill tailings pile. White canyon Wash is in the ribbon of trees just above the tailings pile. The road is going northeast up Farley Canyon.

Photo courtesy of Jack and Melba Winn

White Canyon

4
Robert Stanton and the Glen Canyon Gold Machine

In 1889 an engineer and railroad employee, Robert Brewster Stanton, came to Hite and White Canyon plotting the improbable task of building a railroad down the river. He found and photographed a bustling little mining camp at the mouth of Crescent Creek (North Wash). The camp was about five miles up the river from Cass Hite's store and post office. The miners, with straight faces, called their camp "Crescent City." It had one log cabin, a couple of tents and ten or twelve ragged but eager gold-panning residents.

Robert Stanton wasn't able to build his railroad down the Colorado River. He got sick while in the canyon, an illness called gold-fever. After Cass Hite showed him the Bank of Ticaboo, the promise of treasure hung heavy on his imaginative heart. In the coming years he would spend all of his money, and the money of dozens of other men, in an attempt to tease the yellow gold from the sands of Glen Canyon.

After spending almost ten years drawing up plans, tempting investors and helping to form a company, Stanton was ready to seek his fortune. He had become the brains and guiding light of the Hoskininni Mining Company, named after the old Navajo who told Cass Hite there was gold in the river sand. In 1897 Stanton began work on a magnificent floating dredge.

All materials for the dredge were transported from the railroad siding at Green River to the mouth of Bullfrog Creek. A journey of more than 150 miles in wagons and carts over primitive roads. At Bullfrog, every nut, bolt and board was assembled on a large slip made of pine logs that rested at the water's edge. The behemoth took three years to construct.

The big ship was a floating ore-processing mill designed to dig, segregate and refine the ore-bearing sand and gravels. A huge boom and chain containing 46 large metal digging buckets protruded from the prow. Large amalgamating tables lined with mercury were part of the recovery process, designed to separate and capture the gold.

It was a good plan, but it didn't work. When his steam-powered riverboat-dredge was put in service near the mouth of Bullfrog Creek in 1901, Stanton soon discovered what the low-tech placer miners had known for years. The gold was dust and almost impossible to recover. The yellow dust simply washed back into the river with the tailings and the Hoskininni Mining Company went broke.

White Canyon

Stanton tried to fine-tune the process to make it work, but all of his mechanical expertise, chemical wizardry, hopes, dreams, curses, prayers and good money invested, couldn't fix the problems. Glen Canyon swallowed all of Stanton's money, made a mockery of his ambitions, threw cold water on his plans and sent him back to town humiliated and broke. Just like all the other gold miners in Glen Canyon.

The big dredge was still rusting peacefully in the sunshine when Lake Powell turned the mouth of Bullfrog Creek into Bullfrog Bay some 62-years later. The bones of the wreck still litter the floor of the lake.

The Stanton gold dredge on the Colorado River in 1901
Special Collections P0197, J. Willard Marriott Library, The University of Utah

5
Arth Chaffin and the Hite Ferry

Robert Stanton and the Hoskininni Mining Company abandoned Glen Canyon in 1901. After that, the Colorado River gold rush slowly dissolved and most prospectors went home. Cass Hite died alone in his little cabin in Ticaboo in 1914 at the age of 69. After his death the Hite City Post Office was closed and his store discontinued. His brothers had been helping him run the place, and they too, left the canyons.

It was the early days of the twentieth century and the beginning of a new era. Gold fever had subsided, the prospector camps were gone, and Cass Hite was sleeping in the sand near his Bank of Ticaboo.[1] Glen Canyon was empty and quiet, just the way Cass had found it in 1883.

With the Great Depression of the early 1930s, a man who had been a gold prospector as a boy in the 1890s, and knew the canyons well, came back and bought Cass Hite's old farm and cabins. The year was 1932 and the man was Arthur (Arth) Chaffin. He was there to give gold mining one more chance to make him rich.

Chaffin staked several mining claims up and down the river and dusted-off his gold pan. He also thought he might make a little money by building a ferryboat. People were beginning to travel by automobiles, and they were venturing into the canyons a little more often. Arth decided to entice them. He borrowed road equipment from Garfield County and personally improved the old wagon road down North Wash. The name North Wash had won out over Crescent Creek on the government maps by then.

Arth scratched out a living at Cass Hite's old farm for a number of years. Melons, grapes and fruit grew there in profusion, but transportation was the Achilles heel of the place. It was a long way to markets and the rough roads had a way of turning fruit to jam and melons to juice.

Arth was resourceful and learned to condense and transport some of his wares in pint jars. His "Peach Cordial" elixir became a favorite treat in the back rooms and shady lofts of a few small town connoisseurs. A lot of people during the prohibition years of the 1930s made "home brew" and Arth Chaffin's creations were exceptional. A pint of Peach Cordial went a long way toward sealing agreements, opening doors of opportunity and greasing the wheels of commerce.

Arth tried to strike it rich by panning gold, but for the second time in his life he watched the yellow dust elude his best efforts. He struggled to make a living for years, and as luck would have it, he was in just the right place at the right time when the second gold rush started. In the late 1940s, yellow, gold-colored uranium brought lusty prospectors with stars in their eyes streaming back to the canyons.

Like old Cass Hite, Arth was quick to see a good thing. With a little help from his friends in Hanksville and Blanding, he was able to further improve access to his holdings on the desert. Residents of Hanksville and Blanding were eager to join hands and be good neighbors. One hundred and thirty miles of wilderness stretched between them, and the road was severed by the river. Chaffin was determined to fix that.

With the urging of county commissioners, state legislators, city fathers, good citizens and Arth Chaffin, state road monies became available in 1945 to link Hanksville and Blanding for the first time. The river crossing was a key element in the plans and Arth was proud to do his part. As the bulldozers chewed away at the red rocks and sand, making a new road, Arth was hard at work building a ferryboat.

The new road was dirt and graveled only where absolutely necessary. A few wooden bridges were put in, and a culvert or two. Official state maps warned travelers to carry water and be advised that the road might be impassable due to storms. There were no services on the desert. Everyone knew to carry tools, a shovel, tire chains, an extra fan belt, a blanket, a can of gas, a lunch and big jug of water.

The Hite ferry, or Chaffin Ferry as it was often called, was considered a modern creation. It was constructed of World War II era military pontoon boats lashed together with a plank superstructure. There was a ramp made of planking on each end that could be lowered and raised to allow cars to drive on and off the deck. The vessel was powered by an automobile engine, an antique Model A Ford that drove a series of gears and pulleys attached to a rear wheel that inched the boat along wire-rope cables. The ferry cables spanned the river and hung suspended just above the water.

A closed-circuit telephone was rigged up on the east side of the river where the road ended at the ferry landing. There was a pole there with a phone box attached. Cranking the handle made the phone ring in Chaffin's house across the river. A person could then notify the ferry operator of his wishes to cross over. The person then waited and watched as the ferry crawled along the cable through the water to come and get him. On the west side of the river, people simply knocked on Chaffin's door - if the dogs hadn't summoned the ferry operator already.

Arth Chaffin and the Hite Ferry

The Hite Ferry was put in service on September 17, 1946. Over 400 people came to celebrate with the Chaffins. There were speeches, smiles and non-alcoholic fruit juice and Kool-Aid for everyone. The Governor of the Great State of Utah, Governor Maw, was there to shake hands, kiss babies and take credit for everything. People from Hanksville and Blanding, who only the year before had stood on opposite sides of the river and waved at each other, now shook hands face-to-face and got to know one another.

For the first time ever a person could travel by car from Blanding to Hanksville without going north 130 miles to cross the river bridges at Moab and Green river. The ferry reduced the length of the trip by a third. It also opened new possibilities for commerce, recreation, travel, exploration and sightseeing. To top things off, the timing couldn't have been better. Uranium had recently been discovered in the area.

Arth Chaffin had been there for the gold rush of the 1890s and he knew what was coming. He was standing in the path of a stampede. Every jeep road and sheep trail on the desert bottlenecked at the river and Arth Chaffin was the proud owner of a brand new ferryboat.

The Chaffin (Hite) ferry in 1948. Arth Chaffin digging at left front
Note the antique Model A Ford that provided the engine for the ferry
Photo from the Salt Lake Tribune, January 31, 1988.

White Canyon

The uranium boom is well documented. It left its mark (pun intended) all over the Southwest. A flood of hopeful prospectors invaded the canyons and a uranium mill was constructed at the mouth of White Canyon in 1949. Soon, the little town of White Canyon was a bustling hive of activity. Arth Chaffin had finally found gold in Glen Canyon. He never did get rich, but he made a descent living and saw his dreams fulfilled. Like old Cass Hite, he had made a place for himself in the wilderness he loved and found a way to make other people pay his way. Genius? You bet.

Arth Chaffin ran his ferry for a few years, then leased the ferryboat to others. He was getting to be an old man and he reluctantly moved closer to town. Elmer Johnson ran the ferryboat for a while, then Reed Maxfield, then Ruben Nielsen.

Hite Ferry circa 1954
Orientation is west. Arth Chaffin home at left center.
Photo courtesy of Maurine Dorman

In 1956 work began on the Glen Canyon Dam and the lower canyon began to fill with cement. Arth petitioned the government for compensation for his soon-to-be-drowned Glen Canyon holdings. It became a David and Goliath struggle that lasted for most of the 1960s. In the end, Goliath won. Arth was forced to settle for much less than he thought his properties were worth. Arth Chaffin died in 1979 at the age of 95.

The gates of the Glen Canyon Dam were closed in 1963 and the flood waters of Lake Powell reached upper Glen Canyon in 1964. The Hite ferry site was flooded in June of that year and Arth Chaffin's farm and orchards were abandoned to their fate. A temporary ferryboat was installed near the mouth of North Wash to take construction workers between there and the future site of the Hite Marina. The workers were building the new highway bridges over the Colorado and Dirty Devil Rivers. The temporary ferry remained in service, retreating higher and higher up the canyon walls until the highway bridges were completed in 1966. The last run of the Hite (Chaffin) ferry was on June 5, 1964. When Lake Powell crested in 1980 the water was more than 200 feet deep over Arth Chaffin's ferry moorings and Cass Hite's old log cabin.

Only the name of the place was moved to higher ground. The name was transported five miles up the canyon and taken across the lake to the east side. There the name was given to a concessionaire who used it to help sell gasoline and snow cones to tourists. The Hite Marina wears a name it never earned. Many people who live and work there today don't know the history of its namesake.

Notes:

1. Cass Hite's remains were not relocated before Lake Powell inundated Glen Canyon. He sleeps today under a blanket of cool water.

White Canyon

Hite (Chaffin) Ferry - 1951
Arth Chaffin (far right) shaking hands with Leroy Parker, superintendent
of the White Canyon mill. The other men in hats are Garth and Wells Noyes
Photo courtesy of Maurine Dorman.

6
White Canyon

The little town that grew up across the river from Arth Chaffin's home and Cass Hite's old cabin was named White Canyon. It was on the east side of the Colorado River where White Canyon Wash entered Glen Canyon. The town was planted on a flat place along the river bottom, a quiet river valley boxed in by ledges.

To me, it was the most beautiful place in the world. A place of red rocks and sand with towering bastions of dark sandstone and cream-colored slickrock spilling down into the valley. The sky was bluer there than anywhere else and the cotton ball clouds were cleaner and whiter. A river ran through it, and the sweet, musty smell of the muddy Colorado was always in the air.

The town was named after the deep sandstone canyon in whose rocky mouth she rested. It was an honorable and noble name. White Canyon is one of the gems of the canyon country. A beautiful place with a rich and interesting history.

White Canyon has its roots in the high country of Elk Ridge, almost forty-five miles to the east. The watercourse begins near the Bears Ears, trickling down through the pines and quaking aspen of the rocky heights before spilling over the rim of Elk Ridge toward the desert floor. Almost immediately the canyon is a hundred feet deep. Carved down into the light buckskin-colored sandstone the cowboys call slickrock. The canyon rim is capped with thin red soil and carpeted with cedar and sage. The contrast of the light tan-colored slickrock against the dark red and brown matrix of the surrounding heights, gave the canyon its name. The early pioneers called it White Canyon.

In the upper reaches, White Canyon is narrow and deep, a ragged crack in the crust of the earth. She is only a bow shot wide in some places, but deeper than most city buildings are tall. There are places in the bottom never touched by the sun. The canyon becomes wider and more shallow as it progresses, and in a couple of places dirt roads have been bulldozed from one side to the other. Then, as she nears the Colorado River, White Canyon becomes a deep, narrow crack canyon again.

While rough and imposing, cut down into solid bedrock, White Canyon is a true desert wash and not a stream. There is no constant flow of water through her rocky channel. In the springtime, during snowmelt in the high country, the canyon proudly nurses a weak flow of runoff water all the way to the Colorado. But during late summer, fall and winter, there are long stretches in the canyon where a rabbit can't find enough water to drink.

Upper White Canyon Wash. Bears Ears and Elk Ridge in background.
Natural Bridges National Monument center photo.
Author photo

It seems amazing that such a wondrous place as the White Canyon gorge could have been carved by water. There seems to be so little of it. Yet, the telltale signs are everywhere. Soft sandstone is impressionable and it leaves a record of the floods.

Over countless years, Mother Nature has wrought some impressive monuments into the ribs of the canyon. In the upper reaches, in the shadow of Elk Ridge, there are three spectacular rainbows frozen in stone. The place is called Natural Bridges National Monument. Each sandstone bridge spans most of the length of a football field and they arch over 200 feet into the air. The bridges are truly awe-inspiring. When you stand beneath them you can actually feel their great weight hanging high overhead.

White Canyon

From the bridges, White Canyon continues its way through towering rock formations toward the west. The snow-capped spine of the Henry Mountains shines bright against a blue sky on the western horizon. The Red Rock Plateau is a dark, vertical wall on the left. Several canyons feed in from the right: Deer Canyon, Hideout Canyon, Gravel Canyon, Long Canyon, and Fartknocker (Fortknocker on your map - wink). Al Scorup's irreverent young cowboys had been on the desert far too long when they tagged some of the landmarks with place names. Utah mapmakers have struggled to purge those old, irreverently humorous place names. Molly's Nipple has become Wickiup Peak. Sweet Ass Hills are now Sweet Alice Hills. Shit-a-Ring Canyon is now Shoot-a-Ring Canyon.

But not all cowboy place names were irreverent. In the midst of the feeder canyons, Jacobs Chair presides over the landscape, a great towering throne of sandstone like the Judgment Seat of God. Mossback Butte presides over The Tables of the Sun. Cheesebox Butte is less imposing, reminding travelers of a huge Navajo Hogan.

Twenty miles further down the canyon, the rims become less imposing as the country flattens out. A few miles east of the Hite Marina the view of upper Glen Canyon is spectacular. A great, crested dome, or shield of sandstone marks the skyline above the river. Blue-gray Henry Mountains add depth and texture to the landscape.

Lower White Canyon Wash
View from highway 95 a few miles east of Lake Powell and Hite Marina
Author photo

White Canyon

As she entered Glen Canyon, White Canyon Wash broke free from her confining sandstone walls to flow briefly in a narrow, dirt-banked channel to the river. A weak little trickle of water in the bottom of the wash nurtured a thin strip of willows, tamarisk and weathered old cottonwood trees. The strip of green ended at the riverbank. The Forty-five mile long White Canyon Wash had fulfilled her primeval function, delivering a weak little stream of water to the mighty Colorado River.

From the mouth of White Canyon, a huge sandstone wall can be seen across the river valley to the west. The great wall runs north and south and parallels the course of the river. Along the top of the wall, just south of North Wash, is a barren, orange-colored sandstone rim that looks like it has been all scrunched together and folded like an accordion. My family always called the place, The Wrinkle Rocks.

The Wrinkle Rocks near the mouth of North Wash. Henry Mountains in background. The Colorado River canyon is below the red ledges in the center of the photo. This picture was taken on Highway 95 near the Hite Marina. Note the Hite Marina road at left center.
Author Photo

White Canyon

A few hardy people had lived in the White Canyon area for a number of years. Old Cass Hite of course, and then the Chaffins. Rancher Al Scorup and his bean-eating cowboys camped in caves like the old-time Indians, but they were usually just passing through, chasing cows. Ranch headquarters for the Scorup outfit was on Indian Creek, far away on the north side of Elk Ridge. A hermit named Bert Loper lived twelve miles down the river at the mouth of Red Canyon for a time. Most others were newcomers, including my grandparents. Before the uranium boom, no one had lived at the mouth of White Canyon since the Anasazi disappeared sometime during the dark ages of the thirteenth century.

White Canyon was remote and difficult to get to in the 1950s, but beautiful, and my family loved to be there. There is something spiritual about the red desert that is endearing to people. The place reaches out and takes you in. Once you have experienced the beauty and the essence of the red rocks and canyons, the desert always calls you back.

None of my family lived in that river valley for more than five years. Yet we all look to that place and time as something special. White Canyon is our ancestral home. That warm place by the river is as mystical and as magical as Camelot to some of us, even though we know our feelings supersede the realities. Our family has a special bond, a spiritual kinship in our knowing and remembering the place. Among my people, the memory of White Canyon is a shared communion with nature, God and family.

7
Uranium, the Atomic Monster

Everyone knows the Atomic Age began with a bang. America's top secret *Manhattan Project* during World War II culminated with the use of atomic bombs over Hiroshima and Nagasaki in 1945. What most people don't know is that America had no developed source of uranium anywhere in the country at that time. The story of Uncle Sam's quest for domestic sources of uranium (the Atomic Monster) is a colorful drama, and White Canyon was center-stage.

People had known for a long time there were powerful minerals in paradise. For centuries American Indians had pulverized radioactive carnotite into a scarlet or yellow pigment to be used as body paint. The mineral was highly valued as a trade commodity. Colorful nuclear nuggets of pigment were passed from tribe to tribe across the American Southwest. The indigenous peoples believed there was power in the paint, but they had no clue about how powerful the stuff really was.

In 1871, Dr. Richard Pierce shipped 200 pounds of pitchblende from Colorado to London for experiments with metal alloying, chemical extractions and pigments. The dark mineral intrigued him and he was trying hard to find some useful purpose for the stuff. Pitchblende is a blackish mineral with different physical properties than carnotite. Pitchblende and carnotite both contain uranium compounds and the two minerals would become the primary focus of the twentieth century uranium boom.

At the turn of the twentieth century, the world's first well-known nuclear scientist, Madame Curie, was using Utah ores in her experiments to isolate radium. She had discovered that tiny bullets of atomic particles were shooting out from the minerals and she was trying to capture them and put them to work. Sadly, it took her several years and two Nobel Prizes to discovered that little atomic bullets can be fatal.

Before World War I, vanadium was found to be a good tempering agent in the making of steel. As early as 1912, vanadium was being mined on the San Rafael Swell and the Temple Mountain area of Emery County, Utah. At Temple Mountain, uranium was an unwanted by-product of vanadium mining and was cast aside into refuse piles. Those refuse piles would later jump-start the American nuclear industry.

The atomic bombs dropped on Hiroshima and Nagasaki in 1945 were made with uranium imported from the Belgium Congo (Rwanda) in Africa.

White Canyon

The fact that the United States was not producing its own uranium was not a major concern back then. A little monster dust went a long way and only Americans knew how to use it.

The government first began searching for domestic sources of uranium in 1946, but they sort of kept the lid on things for the first few years. The locations of a few small pockets of radioactive minerals were known, but no one knew how much there really was. The focus was on the western states, and the newly established Atomic Energy Commission secretly sent geologists into the backcountry to make maps and mineralogy surveys to assess the potential.

But even government scientists failed to understand the full promise of atomic energy back then. No one dreamed we would be making tens of thousands of atomic explosive devices in the next few years. If two bombs could bring the Japanese Empire to its knees, surely half-a-dozen would keep the Soviets hiding behind their iron curtain. Few people foresaw that uranium would be the catalyst for a whole new industry.

But then, in 1949, the lid blew off the atomic stew pot. The Russians detonated their own atomic bomb and Americans were suddenly afraid. Almost overnight, thousands of atomic bombs were on the drawing boards and hundreds of ballistic missiles needed shiny new warheads. The Navy began making nuclear engines for submarines and it was now actually possible to make atomic power plants to provide electricity for whole cities. Scientists proclaimed that nuclear engines might actually propel railroad locomotives across the country and starships into the galaxy. And, if it worked for locomotives, submarines and starships, why couldn't the new 1949 Ford be retrofitted with an atomic automobile engine? The possibilities seemed endless.

Uranium was suddenly magic pixie dust. It would solve all of our problems. The radioactive mineral was both the sword to conquer the soviet dragon and the fuel to stoke the fires of industry forever. It was suddenly more valuable than diamonds - and brighter than gold.

After 1949, the government lusted for uranium. In a hurry to stockpile mountains of nuclear wonder dust, the feds recruited the help of the citizenry by dangling the carrot of financial incentives over the canyon country. At first they simply encouraged prospecting and promised to buy the product, but when the flow of uranium remained at only a trickle, they took drastic measures.

In 1951 the government began offering a $10,000 bounty for each significant new find. Five thousand dollars was a reasonably good annual wage back then, and G-men guaranteed minimum ore prices for ten years into the future. By law the government was the only buyer. There was also a formula established where the government would help pay ore transportation costs from mine to mill, depending on the quality of the ore.

The Atomic Energy Commission bulldozed access roads into the backcountry to help with exploration, and they printed and distributed maps and pamphlets with helpful hints for novice prospectors. It was the first and only time the U.S. government actively promoted and participated in a gold rush.

Charlie Steen became the poster boy of the movement when he found the fabulously rich Mi Vida Mine southeast of Moab. He was one of the first men to make multi-millions while prospecting on his own. His rags-to-riches story was told everywhere and he was instantly a national celebrity. Even the government promoted his story as an example of what determined and persevering uranium prospectors could expect. There were fortunes to be made right out there in the dirt. All a man needed was the courage to quit his regular job, invest his life's savings, reach out and make it happen.

Thousands took the bait. Lusty, would-be millionaires claimed and counter-claimed and ripped the earth open for miles around. Seventy years later the land is still marred with holes, tunnels, talus piles, trash, bent drill steels, claim markers and bulldozer tracks - haunting reminders of that frantic search for the Atomic Monster.

Everywhere across the canyon country, irreverent little rock cairns can still be found littering the landscape like piles of fossilized mammoth dung. Many are still holding weather-beaten posts that lean away from the wind. Hidden in the rock piles are rusty tobacco tins or bottles with mummified legal documents inside that give the signatory exclusive rights to the mineral wealth within the prescribed boundaries. They are called claim markers, but most mark only the corners of dreams. People staked claims everywhere and anywhere. Many were speculating, staking a claim just in case someone who knew what he was doing really did find pay dirt nearby.

There was a frenzy of activity all across the desert. Used car salesmen, barbers, short-order cooks and cowboys all quit their jobs and invested everything in a Geiger counter and a camp outfit. Jeeps and pickup trucks beat cow trails into backcountry roads. Tiny, ant-like little humans swarmed over the mesas and towering rock formations, following the needle of their Geiger counter like a ship's compass. Humming little airplanes circled over the desert like vultures, trolling for ore deposits with the latest high-tech electronic wizardry. Geologists pored over maps. Dowsers danced with forked sticks. Lawyers spoke with forked tongues. Drill bits chewed into the sandstone.

Seedy little mining camps sprang up in the canyons everywhere. Dump trucks rattled and bounced over washboardy roads. Miners bladed roads across steep mesa slopes and dynamited tunnels into the ribs of the earth, the offal spilling down onto the valley floors. The gutted mesas could only endure the onslaught, suffering the humiliations in stony silence.

It is said that during the early 1950s, there was more land tied up in mining claims in San Juan County, Utah, than there was land in San Juan County, Utah. 309,380 uranium claims were filed in just four Utah counties between 1946 and 1959. By law, each claim reserved an area 1500 feet by 600 feet, a total of 20.66 acres. Placer, or surface claims tied up 160-acre parcels. Simple mathematics show that the volume of federal land tied up in deep mining claims in Utah alone covered a surface area larger than the state of Vermont. By 1959, almost 12% of all the land in Utah was tied up in uranium claims. By the mid-fifties there were about 800 mines producing high-grade uranium on the Colorado Plateau. The state of Utah alone contributed over nine million tons of high-grade ore to the dawning of the atomic age.

Everyone wanted a piece of the action. Stockbrokers, bankers, land speculators and scam artists had a field day. People in far-off Salt Lake City got rich selling penny stocks and Geiger counters. Dozens of dubious mining companies were organized, some with no assets at all - fronts for selling shares of stock while mining other people's pockets. Men jostled for position and advantage like feeding sharks. Dry holes were "salted" with mill tailings to make the Geiger counters sing, then sold for a few hundred or a few thousand dollars. There were fistfights, shootings and lawsuits. There were claim-jumpers, thieves and dishonest partnerships.

In Moab, "The Uranium Capitol of the World," one controversial player in the atomic intrigues was picked off his front porch by a high-powered rifle from long range. It was a notorious murder that was never solved. All over Utah, lawyers, bankers and hardware stores made money while small-time miners lost everything and fought each other for the scraps.

It was a wild and reckless time out on the desert. The mining industry was virtually unregulated back then. It is amazing from today's perspective to know that government agencies didn't try to stop the vile and thoughtless environmental vandalizing of many of the prospectors and miners.

There were people who simply dropped the blade of a bulldozer and drove from place to place, knocking down trees, ripping up fragile desert landscapes and pushing through Indian mounds, not noticing, or not caring. Trash and empty oil drums were tossed over the rims of canyons to rot in the sun and dissolve into the sand. Broken-down old vehicles were abandoned at the side of the road like worked-to-death old horses.

But the sins of the miners were no different than the Atomic Energy Commission when their people opened access roads on the desert. They too simply bulldozed everything out of the way as they drove caterpillars down the canyon. No environmental or archaeological studies were ever done.

The government was the only buyer of a product being mined on federal land. They could easily have put a lid on the abuses. But scientists and politicians were in a hurry to make lots of bombs and nuclear reactors. They turned a blind eye to the environmental degradation and helped to make it happen. The end justified the means. The Atomic Monster was powerful, worth truckloads of money and more important than the angels of the desert. Every time the monster and the angels wrestled, the monster won. The referees were government agents who looked the other way.

It all came apart like a house of cards in the late 1950s. By then Uncle Sam had uranium coming out of his ears. In 1957 the AEC cut back on the number of tons of ore purchased. In 1958 they quit buying from any new sources and set allotments on production from their long-time suppliers. The writing was on the wall. The small producers were instantly screwed. Small mines worked on short margins and restricted production was a knife in the back that eventually killed them all. In 1962, all bounties and incentives for finding uranium were discontinued.

The industry flared up again in 1966 when it was announced that great quantities of ore would be needed for nuclear power plants. Private companies were also cleared for the first time to purchase uranium directly from the mines and mills. The miners shined up their old tin hardhats and stood by in hopeful anticipation, but it never happened. The government completely quit buying uranium by 1970 and a whole industry rolled over and died. Health, safety and environmental legislation has killed all attempts to resuscitate or jump-start the nuclear industry again. It is now cheaper to import uranium than mine it in our own backyard.

The glory years of the uranium boom were between 1949 and 1954. Those were the years when high-grade ore was found on top of the ground by schoolteachers, cops and rodeo clowns. By 1955 the surface had been combed and the people who were finding monster dust were going deep with drilling rigs. Drilling for uranium is expensive. The little guys stood by with sad faces and empty pockets and watched as the big companies took over. The Atomic Monster had burrowed deep and was now beyond the reach of the common man.

Those brave and pioneer-hearted souls who had shown the courage to chuck it all and invest everything in the dream, trickled back to town like ragged, beaten and retreating soldiers, looking for a new start. Many would never be able to recover their former lives and fortunes.

One of many hundreds of small abandoned uranium mines
in the White Canyon and Glen Canyon areas
Author photo

8
White Canyon Town

The town of White Canyon was born in 1949 when The Vanadium Corporation of America chose the site to build an experimental uranium extraction mill. The site offered many advantages. It was central to the mining district. There was water nearby. The state of Utah maintained the road. The ferryboat was a necessary transportation link. There was a long stretch of flat ground suitable for an airfield. And, the winters were mild. The site was also smack in the middle, halfway between Hanksville and Blanding, the two little towns anchoring the ends of a primitive dirt road that passed through the area.

The mill processed ore from the Happy Jack Mine that burrowed deep into the ribs of the Red Rock Plateau, just a few miles up the canyon toward Blanding. Happy Jack ore was contaminated with copper and small amounts of gold. The impurities presented special challenges for the times. They were difficult to separate from the uranium. The White Canyon mill was set up to solve the problems and develop a cost-effective and practical process.

The Happy Jack began life as a copper mine. The owners knew there was uranium in the ore, but it was considered an impurity and a waste product. Uranium got in the way of copper mining in the same way uranium got in the way of vanadium mining on Temple Mountain. Because of bad roads and long distances to copper smelters, the copper mine failed to show a profit and sat idle for many years.

In 1946, Joe Cooper and Fletcher Bronson, farmers and construction workers from Monticello, Utah bought the mine for one thousand dollars and formed the Bronson and Cooper Mining Company. What happened to the partners in the next few years might have been dumb luck, or it might have been calculated foresight, people disagree. Perhaps it was fate.

Either way, their timing was very good. By 1948 copper contaminated with uranium was suddenly uranium contaminated with copper. They were among the first in the nation to own a high-grade uranium mine and they made millions. Agents from the newly created Atomic Energy Commission came courting with flowers, champagne and a bottomless checkbook.

Partners Cooper and Bronson ran the mine for ten years, lining their nests with golden straw while basking in the warm glow of radioactive sunbeams. They waxed fat. Federal agents stood by in black tie and tails and scurried to do their bidding. The partners sold the mine to the Texas Zinc Minerals

White Canyon

Corporation in 1956 for ten million dollars and rode off into the sunset happy. For the second time in their short mining career, their timing was perfect. The next year, 1957, things started to go downhill.

An early photo of the White Canyon Town and mill site taken in 1949. Orientation is northwest looking up the Colorado River. The large rock building at left center is an impressive, ancient Anasazi ruin called Fort Moki. The buildings at lower right are part of the uranium mill, still under construction. Note the cars parked in front of the tree line that marks the boundaries of White Canyon Wash. Beyond the tree line is the "civilian" side of town where mill workers with families would built temporary homes or park camp trailers. Most had yet to arrive when this photo was taken. The upper tree line is the mouth of Farley Canyon where the road to Blanding turned east and disappears from this photograph. Note the road going up the canyon below the hills. The airfield is to the left of that road on the long stretch of flat ground.

Photo courtesy of Dan Marsing

The mill at White Canyon was a pilot plant, a small experimental unit. The mill took limited amounts of ore from small independent mines in the area, but the bulk of the ore came from the Happy Jack. The mill processed

26,358 tons of raw ore between April 1949 and the end of December 1953. 128,145 pounds (64 tons) of uranium sodium diuranate was extracted and sold to the Atomic Energy Commission during the life of the mill.

The mill broke the raw ore down into a thick, rich "yellowcake" that was about 80% pure and more radioactive than the sands of Alamogordo. The concentrate was sealed in 350 lb. metal casks and transported by trucks to Durango for further processing. It was a journey of more than 200 miles and the first 75-mile leg of the trip was over a rough and washboardy dirt and gravel road. The dust-covered, vibration-numbed truck drivers didn't see asphalt until they crawled up on highway 191 near Blanding.

The beginnings of the White Canyon mill and town circa 1949. The boarding house is the larger building back against the trees of White Canyon Wash. Tent-cabins for the mill workers were not constructed at the time this photo was taken. The Hite ferry landing was to the left of this photo about half-a-mile down the river bank.
Courtesy of Dan Marsing

White Canyon

White Canyon mill near the end of construction - 1949
Courtesy of Dan Marsing

White Canyon Town was like a lighthouse beacon during the boom years between 1949 and 1954. She was born, lived and died by uranium and she was many things to many people. The town became an economic gold mine for the sons of Mormon pioneer farmers who lived in neighboring little towns. A supply depot for weather-beaten prospectors. A desert oasis for weary travelers. A ragged Bedouin camp in the eyes of high class city dwelling visitors. A surrogate home for most townspeople. And Grandma's house to little boys. The mill was a generous employer of semi-skilled hands and a wilderness shrine to the Atomic Monster.

The nation had became highly militarized during the years of World War II and that mindset carried over to the search for uranium. Atomic power was the legacy and an extension of the conflicts of the second world war. Finding and processing fuel for atomic bombs was a patriotic thing to do. Like Rosie the Riveter, uranium workers were civilians serving in the age-old conflict between good and evil. The Soviet menace could be kept in check only by building hundreds of atomic bombs. It was a pact with the devil, but considered worth the risks.

White Canyon Town

White Canyon Town was a pharmacy where radioactive monster dust was transformed by alchemy into a magic golden powder that was sent to white-smocked scientists in secret labs in secret facilities. The scientists took the radioactive magic powder and experimented with recipes in boiling caldrons that held the fate of the world.

The uranium mill at White Canyon was remarkably unimposing as an agent of such awful power. It looked like a disorganized collection of buildings, smoke stacks, holding tanks, acid baths, leaching tables, conveyor belts and catwalks. The mill was unpainted, unadorned, and looked rusty and crude. The place looked more like a train wreck than an important nuclear facility. The mill rumbled, growled and belched steam and smoke as it chewed and digested the rich and spicy uranium ore. Mineral waste from the facility was stacked-up in the dooryard like a manure pile near a stable. Smokestacks vented vile, acid-soaked gasses out into the unsuspecting sunshine.

And yet … some of us loved the place. The little town had many redeeming features. Her hands may have been dirty but her heart was clean. There was an endearing innocence about her. She was caught up in the excitement of the quest for uranium and the workers truly believed she was part of something great and noble. The focus of the whole nation was atomic energy and White Canyon Town was the very heart of the action. Most, if not all of the workers, were proud to be there.

The technology of the mill was state-of-the-art and the disposal of waste was within accepted parameters of the laws and consciousness of the nation at the time. There was no wicked plot to foul the environment and poison the air and water. It's just that people didn't know any better. The good citizens and their government accepted a lower standard as normal. Mining and milling was dirty business. The gas, dust and noise was accepted as a necessary blight. No one really expected companies to spend large amounts of money to clean things up. There was no profit in that. Mines and mills everywhere fouled their nests. Workers and neighbors lived with it. Things had always been that way.

A boardinghouse and a row of worker's billets spread out on the red sand at the foot of the uranium mill. The buildings were a series of crude little cabins with plank floors and walls of rough-cut pine boards. The roofs and exterior walls were covered with rolled asphalt tarpaper to seal the cracks between the boards. The cabins squatted in the dirt without the dignity of proper cement foundations. The buildings were unpainted and weathering in the sun. There was no grass, sidewalks or landscaping anywhere.

White Canyon

The cabins were field expedient barracks, a military-inspired solution. They were a cheap way to accommodate a transient workforce for a relatively short period of time. The place looked like an army camp on the sands of North Africa during the war. Each of the cabin-billets housed two men and there were about a dozen of them stretched out in a long, straight line toward the river. They were equipped with military surplus bunks and army footlockers for personal gear.

The cookhouse, or boardinghouse as it was called, was also a cabin of the same rough-cut material as the billets, only larger and with long tables and benches to seat the clientele. In keeping with the military feel of the place, the boardinghouse had a sign over the door that said, "Mess Hall."

The uranium mill, boardinghouse, cabin-billets, bathhouse, and an odd collection of outbuildings were on the south side of White Canyon Wash. They made up the company side of town. The buildings paralleled the creek, arranged in a long, straight row, disciplined and orderly. It looked as though a good First Sergeant had supervised the construction.

On the north side of White Canyon Wash, a store, one-room school, assorted cabins, camp trailers and dozens of sheds and outbuildings made up the civilian side of town. The undisciplined civilians were scattered haphazardly. No military decorum there. A narrow bridge of thick wooden planking, suitable for dump trucks, spanned White Canyon Wash and joined the two sides of town.

The airstrip paralleled the river. A windsock marked the southern terminus about half-a-mile above the store. The northern end of the runway was lost somewhere in the distant sand and sage that stretched up the canyon.

White Canyon Town was not a true town in the usual sense of the word. There were no churches, parks, pavement, sidewalks or cemeteries. She was a boomtown, thrown together to serve the uranium industry and the prospectors who frequented the area at the time. It was a community of transients drawn together by good-paying jobs and dreams of hitting it big during weekend excursions into the canyons. Every man owned his own Geiger counter. It was a hard working little place, not like the rowdy mining camps from another century. Most of the men had their families there. And, though the town had no churches, there were no saloons, gambling dens or dance hall girls either … at least not officially.

There were less than a dozen little tarpaper houses in town and the population never exceeded 250 people. Single men lived in the military billets or camped out. Most families lived in cramped little camp trailers or improvised shed-houses and endured. The whole town seemed to be living with their bags packed and ready to move on.

A man named Myron Ferre (he pronounced his last name "Free") controlled almost everything in town. He was an entrepreneur from Grand Junction, Colorado and one of the few men to find gold in Glen Canyon. The gold he found was in other people's pockets. He mined it with enthusiasm and imagination. He owned the town's only store and the town's only gas pump. He was the postmaster and ran the post office from his home. He rented camp trailers and trailer-spaces to prospectors and transient mill workers. He tapped and sold clean water to the townsfolk, supervised a poor-boy automotive garage, and sold electricity from his private diesel generator.

The town had an official post office and "White Canyon, Utah" was a legitimate address on an envelope, but the town was unincorporated and had no official Mayor or city council. Company officials at the mill were the unofficial city fathers. But in spite of all that, Myron Ferre was everywhere and involved in everything. He was a one-man chamber of commerce, maintenance department, utilities supervisor, sanitation department, animal control officer, social services provider and credit union. He offered valuable goods and services way out there on the lonesome desert. He was much appreciated and respected.

The town had no paved streets, sidewalks, lawns, streetlights, telephones, indoor plumbing, radio, TV, movie theaters, or hamburger joints. There was no official policeman, fire department or medical infirmary. Myron Ferre's diesel generator was shut down at ten o'clock at night, ready or not, and everyone had a coal oil lamp and a flashlight ready to take over. In many ways it was like living in the 1800s.

There was a one-room schoolhouse in town that served the needs of about forty students. Ages and grade levels varied greatly. Townspeople struggled and sacrificed to keep the school viable. It was a bare bones and no-nonsense little place. School kids spent recess chasing lizards, throwing rocks and playing in the dirt of the schoolyard. There was no grass or playground equipment, no gymnasium, cafeteria, school buses or free lunch. There was also no audio-visual equipment. Students toured the world in books and learned to read.

Boys and girls went to school wearing scrubbed faces and their best shoes. Girls wore pressed and pleated skirts, of course, anything less would have been barbaric. School was a special place in the 1950s. Kids paid respect by dressing as well as when they went to church, even at the one-room schoolhouse in White Canyon. Male schoolteachers always wore neckties and women teachers always wore skirts. Public education had a different feel in those days. It was a privilege and an opportunity.

Dee Johnson, Jeanie Foster and Elaine Foster at the White Canyon School
Courtesy of Jeanie Foster McDoniel

Good teachers were hard to find out there in the boondocks. There is a story about a schoolteacher who came to White Canyon as one of those bold and brave-hearted souls who had thrown it all away to chase the Atomic Monster. The man had been the principal of a high school in a big city and had given it up to cast his fate on the desert sands. He limped into town discouraged and beaten, his grubstake and his energy all used up and gone. Teaching was probably the only job in town that rose to the level of his education. He signed on to run the one-room school for a while. In a sad attempt to restore lost titles and glory, he always referred to himself as the "principal" of the little school and not the teacher. Experienced teachers were hard to come by, so the good citizens only smiled as they indulged his vanity.

A group of children at the White Canyon School.
Back row left to right: Elaine Foster, Sally Brown, Richard Crawford, Don Brown. Middle row: Ray Seager, unknown, (?) Crawford, (?) Crawford, Johnny Marsing. Bottom row: Susie Brown, Connie Marsing, Shanna Seager.
Courtesy of Jeanie Foster McDoniel

Pearl Baker was also the schoolteacher for a while. She was a daughter of the desert, without a teaching credential or higher education, but she accepted the challenge and did a good job. She later wrote some very interesting and entertaining books about her early life and adventures in the Robber's Roost Country of Emery County. Her father was Charlie Bittlecomb, the pioneer rancher who moved onto the Robber's Roost in 1912 to start a cattle operation that eventually became the famous Ekker Ranch.

The schoolhouse was also the community meeting hall and sometimes dances were held there. The whole town would turn out and it was crowded in the little one-room building. Little boys had to squeeze into a corner to watch without being stepped on. Music was provided by a scratchy old record player and there was a shortage of female dance partners. The men had a broom they passed around. A man would cut in on a dancing couple by tapping the other man on the shoulder and exchanging the broom for the hand of the girl. It was a big joke to see who got stuck with the broom at the end of the dance. That broom changed partners like it was too hot to touch. People knew how to have fun in those days and no one was left out.

Church was held in the schoolhouse on Sunday mornings too. White Canyon was in the heart of Mormon country and most of the townsfolk were Mormons. In keeping with Mormon tradition, a worthy and respected member of the little congregation was called by church authorities to be the "Presiding Elder." A very young Dan Marsing was Presiding Elder for several months, and after he was drafted to serve his country during the Korean War, my Uncle, Var Winn, was temporarily pressed into service as shepherd of the little flock. The White Canyon Branch of the church was an extension of the Hanksville Ward, about 70 miles away. Bill Wells was Hanksville's "Flying Bishop" and the regional presiding authority. Bishop Wells flew into town often to officiate in church business.

Like most other little towns isolated on the desert, the church was the social center as well as the spiritual core of the community. Someone had dragged an old piano out there on the desert and it became the centerpiece for the little school, turned church, turned community meeting place and dance hall.

Bill Wells, the flying Bishop, was southern Utah's Mormon St. Christopher, the patron saint of travelers on the desert skies. He was an angel of mercy who came on silver wings to take sick and injured people to the doctors or ferry people to and from White Canyon for family emergencies. He often donated his time and his flying machine to search for lost Boy Scouts, stranded prospectors and river drowning victims. He helped the county sheriff track bad guys and he rented his services to mining companies, government agents and wealthy sightseers. His little plane was always busy. It knew all of the trails in the sky out over the desert.

White Canyon Town

There was not a telephone in that whole section of southern Utah. Emergency communication with the rest of the planet was conducted by a citizen-band radio that cast long beams down the valley and through the maze of canyons. The radio waves reached out and lightly tickled the distant receivers in Bryce Canyon National Park about ninety air miles away. The radio operator in Bryce Canyon then made a long-distance telephone call back to Hanksville to summon Bishop Wells. Bill Wells then flew to White Canyon and dropped his little plane onto the dirt runway to make the pick-up or delivery. It was a triangle of long-distant communication that spanned many miles and many precious minutes - sometimes hours or days - depending on weather and atmospheric conditions. It was a primitive and inefficient system, especially when someone was in pain, or bleeding.

The gathering place in White Canyon Town was Myron Ferre's little store that stood behind the gas pump on the civilian side of town. The store, or, White Canyon Trading Post, as a stenciled sign proclaimed, was a modest affair and stocked primarily with necessities. Gasoline and supplies were trucked in over the long and bumpy roads from the edges of civilization and the price of goods reflected the journey. The store was also the only building in town with swamp cooler air-conditioning. Townspeople congregated there like a herd of sheep under a lone cottonwood tree, seeking shelter from the sweltering desert heat.

The Store and Post Office in White Canyon – under construction in 1950
Courtesy of Dan Marsing

White Canyon

It has been said, that for a few years, the White Canyon Store might have sold more beer than any other store, bar or liquor outlet in Utah. It was the only watering hole in hundreds of miles and thirsty miners and sun-parched prospectors bought beer by the case and not by the can. In seedy little mining camps all over the desert, beer was stockpiled like drill steels and dynamite.

Drinking beer was a manly, honorable form of entertainment in the isolation of the desert. Digging for pay dirt gave a man a powerful thirst. Besides, there was little to do after work. The town had no TV or movie theaters, no dance halls, public library or social clubs, not even AM radio reception. In the cool of the evenings the rattling sound of empty beer cans being scoop-shoveled into the wash behind the store could be heard all over town.

All trash from town was thrown into White Canyon Wash behind the buildings. It collected there, rusting and festering, sometimes for months. The improvised, open-air dump collected flies and opportunistic rodents. The garbage melted into the banks of the streambed until one of those blessed little desert storms scoured the dusty slickrock of the White Canyon drainage. When the floodwater came crashing down the canyon, it bulldozed the trash out into the river where it sank and disappeared.

A single ribbon of dirt road snaked down from Farley Canyon and bumped through town. The dusty trail was anchored in Blanding, and in White Canyon it served as Main Street. The road wandered through town, crossed the wooden White Canyon Bridge, passed by the boardinghouse and the mill and ended at the ferryboat landing on the riverbank. All through-traffic had to cross the river on the boat. On the west side of the river, at Hite, the road continued its course toward the Henry Mountains and Hanksville, wending its way up and out of North Wash.

The ferryboat was a bridge that held eastern Utah and western Utah together. A cargo ship that brought mill supplies and spare parts from Provo and Salt Lake, and groceries and dry goods from Price and Green River. The boat swam the muddy river with its plank decking high and dry, carrying cars and trucks, mill workers, cowboys and prospectors, government functionaries, sightseers, and happy little boys eager to visit Grandma.

The airfield was also a critical link to the little community. The mail was flown in a couple of times a week. Emergency supplies and vital spare parts for the mill were usually transported by air. When medical emergencies happened, Bishop Wells' little airplane served as an ambulance.

White Canyon Town

The airstrip was a long, bulldozed swath through the sand and bushes along the riverbank. There was no aircraft hanger, control tower or runway lights. No buildings at all in fact. The only aid to takeoffs and landings was a windsock that sagged from a tall metal pole at the south end of the field. The small aircraft that used the landing strip were parked out on the dirt and tethered to the ground with cables and ropes. The pilots had learned to tie the planes down after a strong canyon wind overturned a couple of them unexpectedly one cloudy afternoon. From town, a person could usually see two or three airplanes staked to the ground while waiting patiently near the end of the runway. The little airplanes always looked droopy and tired, sleeping in the warm sunshine like saddle horses tied to a hitching rail.

Then, there were the people. The town of White Canyon and the people who lived there were making history, and they knew it. There was an attitude about the place, a feeling of purpose and excitement always in the air. But then, the 1950s were like that everywhere. The war was over. America had saved the world from tyranny and she was proud. It was America's time in the spotlight on the world stage and Americans everywhere walked tall.

After the war, Americans were united in purpose and excited by the possibilities that lay before them. A dynamic middle class was sprouting from the fears and tears of the great depression and the ashes of the second world war. Manufacturing, mining, milling and farming were all vibrant and vital homeland industries. There were good jobs with good pay and good benefits for everyone. The future was without limits.

In White Canyon Town, the prospectors, miners, mill workers, truck drivers and company officials all thought of themselves as American patriots. The A-bomb was a good thing in the early fifties. Nuclear power was the key to the future. They were all proud to be a part of it.

People in the uranium industry were on the cutting-edge of technology and patriotic morality. They were trailblazers and pioneers on a new frontier and they were leading us into a brave new world. They were soldiers, out to save the world from the horrors of war by making explosive devices too terrible to ever be used. They were conservationists, offering atomic energy as a way to save other, less valuable natural resources. They were good citizens, answering a call to find, process and stockpile that most valuable of radioactive minerals, and they were proud. The uranium workers always stood tall in their tin hard-hats. They were well paid and well respected.

In was early 1952 when my maternal Grandmother, Bertha Winn, contracted to run the boardinghouse in White Canyon. My Grandfather, Lorin Winn, and three of my uncles took jobs working at the uranium mill. I was five years old when my family first went there. Brother Reed was three. We never lived there full-time like our grandparents and extended family, but we visited often. Reed was there more often than I. By the end of the second summer I was a big boy with responsibilities. I was in the first grade at Wellington Elementary.

9
The Boardinghouse

When Lorin and Bertha Winn migrated to White Canyon, the town was three years old and at its high point. It was early 1952 and the place was a hive of activity. The uranium mill hummed and clanked and chewed up tons of high-grade ore. Dump trucks clattered over washboardy roads, kicking up clouds of red dust while caterpillars and front-end loaders pushed piles of ore and mill tailings around and around. Jeeps and pickup trucks were parked at odd angles and in odd places all over town. Fragile little airplanes buzzed the mill before lightly touching down in the dust of the airfield. Arth Chaffin's ferryboat swam back and forth across the river, bravely breasting the waves and smiling the whole time.

Lorin and Bertha took up residency at the boardinghouse on the company side of town. It was the center of all the action. Myron Ferre's air-conditioned store was the most popular place in White Canyon, but the boardinghouse was more important. The boardinghouse was where the company big shots took their meals and where many of them hung out in the evenings. It was an informal company lounge, a substitute office building, recreation center, employment office, visitor's center, information bureau and coffee shop. The "Mess Hall" was company owned and the clientele were members of an exclusive club.

The Vanadium Corporation had several men without wives and families working at the mill and living in the company-owned cabins. The company provided the boardinghouse as a place where those men could take their meals. Some men had children attending schools in other towns and were reluctant to uproot and transplant them to the little one-room school in the canyon. This meant that some families were separated for weeks or months at a time. Working at the mill was good, high-paying and steady employment, and some family's thought the separation was worth the material benefits.

Most family men brought their wives and children to White Canyon. They lived on the civilian side of town and rented trailers or trailer space from Myron Ferre. Some, who expected to be there for a while, built their own little tarpaper houses or brought in trailers of their own. Families were not allowed to live in the company-owned billets and they could not use the boardinghouse on a routine basis.

My grandparents were different. Bertha was under contract to the company and housing was part of the deal. She and Grandpa were assigned one of the tarpaper-covered cabins to live in. Grandma was the only woman who lived full-time on the company side of town.

Boarding House at White Canyon, 1952. Left to right, Lorin Winn, Bertha Winn, Lorraine Winn Noyes, Jack Winn, Mel Young
Courtesy of Maurine Dorman

As matron of the boardinghouse, Bertha served three meals a day, seven days a week. It was a daunting task and a backbreaking schedule. There was no time off. She had to get up early to get breakfast started. She peeled potatoes, cut meat, cracked eggs, made bread and pies, scrubbed floors and washed all the dishes by hand. The cooking was done over a propane stove and dishes were washed in a deep sink. She did have running water tapped into the kitchen. The drain was a hose that snaked into White Canyon Wash behind the building. A huge diesel generator at the mill supplied electricity. The mill supplied power to all of the company buildings and there were stark, uncovered light bulbs dangling from insulated wiring in all of the cabin-billets.

Grandma's eighteen-year-old and newly married daughter, Lorraine, helped her most of the time. Lorraine lived on the other side of town, but she spent most of her time at the boardinghouse helping her mother. They served as many as twenty men plus their own husbands at each meal. The company charged mill workers a monthly fee to eat at the boardinghouse. Visitors, usually big shots from the company, consulting engineers, vendors, or government functionaries, paid by the meal. Bertha received a monthly salary. Lorraine worked for free, just to help her mother.

Inside the boardinghouse, the air was always sweet with the smell of baking bread. Great kettles of simmering stew, potatoes, spaghetti, or ham and lima beans crowded the propane stovetop. The wooden bench-tables and the plank floor always seemed to be dark and still wet from a good scrubbing, and the scent of wet wood and soap struggled to be noticed through the smells of the cooking. Heat from the stove joined the hot desert air to turn the dampness into steam and the place sweltered. Grandma wiped her face with a frilly handkerchief she kept in the pocket of her apron. A large electric fan tried to help, but only stirred the hot, damp air.

Grandma hurried from task to task wearing her long apron and housedress, her graying hair pinned back and out of her face. She cooked while her pretty young daughter sat on a wooden bench with a paring knife carving up a mountain of potatoes, one potato at a time. They were feeding strong and hard-working young men who could put away a lot of groceries. The workers expected, and got, high-calorie and high-octane food. Thin soup and crackers wouldn't do. The mill workers lived on meat and potatoes with homemade bread and pie. Grandma bought groceries by the truckload and she kept the road to Price dusted in the effort.

There was a very large, restaurant-style coffee maker in the boardinghouse that would hold a few dozen cups. The big coffee pot was the social center on the company side of town, both in the mornings and evenings. Folgers and MJB jump-started everyone's heart in the mornings, and filled tired bellies with warm liquid before the workers dropped off to sleep in the evenings. The company coffeepot was, without a doubt, the most valuable and necessary modern convenience between Blanding and Hanksville.

Unfortunately, Grandma was a Mormon Saint who never touched coffee. It was against her religion. She let it be known right away that she didn't use the stuff, didn't need the stuff and wouldn't touch the stuff.

Fortunately, Grandpa was a connoisseur who drank the nectar of the beans by the quart. He gallantly stepped in and saved her from her dilemma. Grandpa became the alchemist who knew the secret recipe for the big pot, and he kept the kettle brewing day and night.

White Canyon

The boardinghouse had a refrigerator and a deepfreeze, but it was still a challenge to store and keep enough meat, milk and eggs to serve forty to sixty meals every day. There were few vendors willing to brave the caravan routes that were the lifeline to the little town, and Grandma had to make-do as best she could. Family members made full-truck grocery runs to the pantries of civilization on a routine basis.

They often bought a whole beef or pork and cut it up themselves, and they used a great deal of condensed, canned milk. It was difficult to get frozen foods to White Canyon too. It took hours over the rough roads to make the trip and picnic coolers were still somewhere in the future. Frozen meat and vegetables were wrapped in paper, packed in cardboard boxes, covered with a tarp, and the delivery driver drove as fast as he could over the rough roads.

Sometimes they bought dry ice from the ice plant in Wellington to pack frozen foods. Dry ice had to be handled carefully. It would freeze-burn things in direct contact, and it could not be sealed tight or the escaping gasses would build pressure and blow things up.

A bonus to using dry ice was that a chunk of the leftover stuff could be saved to make a big batch of homemade root beer. All that was needed was a bottle of root beer extract, sugar, dry ice, and a ten or twenty gallon metal can of water to mix it in. The dry ice chilled and carbonated the drink as it dissolved in the liquid. The root beer bubbled and splashed as the gas escaped, and a thick vapor spilled down the outside of the can and spread over the floor as the caldron boiled. Exciting stuff for little boys. The root beer was good too, and a real treat in a town without an ice-cream shop. When the word got out that Grandma was making root beer at the boardinghouse, half the town would show up with big smiles and tin cups.

Fragile products like eggs and glassware were always a challenge on the rough roads and had to be packed carefully. There were no plastic food containers in those days. Milk, ketchup, mayonnaise, sauces, syrup, jam and dozens of other things came packaged in glass jars. The fragile nature of the cargo was one of the reasons it usually took five hours or more to drive the 170 miles between Price and White Canyon. Hauling boxes of glass-encased cargo over the rough desert roads was like riding a roller coaster with a raw egg in your hand.

Often, mischievous little boys lurked in the boardinghouse kitchen, getting in the way and competing with the potatoes for Grandma's attention. A favorite game was to sneak up on the stove and steal a slice of frying potato without being caught, or to reach across the table and snatch a piece of recently sliced homemade bread. Grandma would wrinkle her brow and wave a big spoon threateningly, and then she would smile and butter the bread for us, sometimes giving us a hug or a pat on the head in the bargain.

Outside, through the screen doors that kept the flies and mosquitoes at bay, the desert locusts hummed happily in the twisted cottonwoods. The boarding house was set back against the trees and the wash as far as possible as if trying to steal just a little shade. The cottonwoods were stingy with their shade, and most of it spilled down into the creek bottom and was wasted on the frogs and locusts.

The desert locusts (Katydids) lived in the cool and shady branches and the air around the boardinghouse was often filled with the music of their song. They made a noise similar to crickets, only louder and with an amplified buzz to it. It was a vibrant and pulsating chorus that filled the air with a background noise like radio static. The happy little bugs serenaded the bustle of the little town all through the day. They hummed their little hearts out until evening shadows crept over the valley floor, then they stepped aside as a choir of frogs took over to do the night shift.[1]

The buzz and hum of the big bugs was always in the air. And when the insects were disturbed by some loud noise or a sudden shift in the wind, and stopped their singing for only a moment, it was as if the desert air was sucked back into the vacuum of the silence. The whole town stopped and held its breath, and listened. Then, when the bugs started singing again, everything returned to normal. All was well.

At dinnertime the mill workers came to the boardinghouse and Grandma had the long bench-tables all set. She had bright oilcloth table coverings, and sometimes handfuls of desert flowers, pussy willow, or October tinted cottonwood leaves in mason jars as table decorations. Grandma always went an extra mile and tried hard to make the boardinghouse a pleasant place to eat.

I don't know what those men paid for each meal, but it wasn't enough. Grandma was to cooking what Michelangelo was to painting and sculpting. She was a Master. Even her potato soup would take you to Nirvana. Her hot biscuits would melt on your tongue. Her carrot cake and warm cinnamon rolls simply stopped your clock.

Little boys took naps during the day and Grandma would lay us out on her bed in the rough-board cabin and then return to her duties. The billets always had dim, shady interiors. There were no windows that I can remember, but a screen door at each end of the building kept us in touch with what was going on outside. We would lie on Grandma's soft bed in the dim light and listen to the hum of the mill, the rattle of dump trucks and the buzz of the desert locusts. It all blended into a lullaby and we were soon fast asleep.

White Canyon Town had a smell to it, different from other towns. The smell was especially noticeable in the hot shade of the cabins during the heat of the day. There was always the musty, wet-boot smell of the river of course, and the dry, pollen-dusted scent of the tamarack bushes. But there was also the smell of oil, diesel smoke and hot tar.

Near the mill were large, dark stains in the sand where oil had been drained onto the ground as company mechanics serviced equipment. Sometimes the heat shimmering air above the oil stains had a hazy, bluish tint to it. Also, empty oil drums, cans and spent oil filters were usually discarded in the weeds or stacked in the bushes. The sticky, oily residues scorched in the sun and cooked in the dark, open metal containers. At the cabins, hot tar oozed from black tarpaper walls and asphalt roofing as the sun beat down. The oily, hydrocarbon smell filled the cabins in the daytime, and the whole town smelled like the inside of an old automobile repair shop.

Sometimes little boys played outside in the dooryard of the boardinghouse. We tromped through the sand and chased grasshoppers and lizards in the weeds. White Canyon grew the world's best lizards and some of them were Boone and Crockett contenders. Some grew over a foot long and must have weighed more than a pound. Some of the big ones even worked-out to keep in shape. The husky lizards would set out on flat rocks in the mornings and do push-ups while they checked out the new day and waited for the lady lizards to pass by. It was fun to watch.

Some of the lizards had yellow bellies, some had red bellies, and some were plain old gray or white-bellies. We chased and tormented those. But we always ran away from the blue-belly lizards. We knew that blue-bellied lizards were poisonous. I don't know how we knew that, but finding a blue-belly lizard was like encountering a rattlesnake to us kids and we always ran away from them. Nothing was ever more dangerous or more poisonous than a dreaded blue-bellied lizard. Where we got that notion, I haven't a clue.

One day, Mr. Parker, the mill superintendent and the most important man in town, was ambushed by a fat lizard right on the doorstep of the boardinghouse. The boardinghouse had a single step made from a flat rock. Mr. Parker was walking up to the door to talk to Grandma and the big lizard shot out from under the building and zipped right up his pant leg.

Mr. Parker was motivated and he headed the intruder off just in the nick of time, grabbing him just short of his crotch. He pinned the reptile in a wad of pant leg and held the struggling trespasser in a death-grip. Without hesitating, he quickly opened his pants to the bright sunshine and Grandma's shocked, piously innocent and open-mouthed gape. He fished the disgusting and struggling little beast out of his boxers and flung the semi-squashed lizard out into the bushes. He then turned and went his way, redoing his britches while trying to pretend that nothing unusual had happened. His ears glowed red as he walked away, and Grandma turned blue before she had the presence of mind to exhale.

It was a little while before Mr. Parker came back to finish his business at the boardinghouse. By then, the natural color of his face and his proper superintendent's decorum had been restored to normal. Grandma didn't recover quite as easily. She talked to him with a straight and poker-playing face, but with glowing cheeks and a severely repressed smile. I'm sure her eyes gave her away.

I never got to see the lizard that blazed the trail up Mr. Parker's hairy leg, but I knew darn well that it had to be one of those dreaded blue-bellied devils.

Mr. Parker was the Big Cheese in White Canyon Town. He was the mill superintendent and the guy who hired and fired all of the mill workers. The unofficial Mayor of Paradise. He was an older man, probably in his sixties, and he seemed to be a nice guy. My grandparents both worked for him and they always called him Mister Parker, even when he wasn't there. I didn't know until years later that his given name was Leroy.

My grandparents were proud and independent people and they considered themselves the equal of almost anyone. They didn't call many people "Mister." For a long time I thought they were just kissing-up to Mister Parker because he was the boss. But later, I came to understand that it was something beyond that. The man had truly won their respect and admiration. Many years later, and a long time since the man had held any sway or power over them, they still talked affectionately of "Mister Parker," the mill superintendent. I wish I could have known the man. He must have been someone special.

There was a magnificent Indian ruin above town on a high bluff that looked out over the river canyon. It was the most famous ruin in all of Glen Canyon. John Wesley Powell had described it, measured it and sketched it into his journals in 1869. Early prospectors and miners had christened it Fort Moki. I don't remember people calling the ruin Fort Moki when I was a kid. It was always "the Indian fort" to us. Moki was the name most people from the southeast Utah used for the Anasazi back then.

White Canyon

The ruin was impressive. It towered over the little town and it was obviously a fort. It was on the perfect vantage point to command the whole valley. Nothing could move below but what a sharp-eyed sentry would see. The fort dominated the valley and the ancient Indian trail up White Canyon Wash. It was the perfect spot for stone-age defenders to vanquish stone-age attackers.

Fort Moki stood as sentinel over the little valley that housed the White Canyon Town site. The ruin was on a rocky promontory 100 feet above the canyon floor and was the most famous ruin in all of Glen Canyon before Lake Powell. Compare this photo to the JWP sketch on page 6.

Author photo - December 1959

The ruin stood as a silent witness, watching generations of men come and go in the valley below. She had endured centuries of searing desert sun, cold winter winds, vandals, treasure hunters, and a complete lack of maintenance. And yet, her walls still towered bold and strong. She still held the high ground, like any good fort or temple, and she looked down on the world bravely as her strong walls held up the desert sky.

The Boardinghouse

My first visit to that ancient fort was an epiphany for me, a true spiritual awakening. I was only six years old, yet deeply moved as I explored that ruin. The majesty and the mystery of the place overwhelmed me. The ruin had a feel that was different from anything I had ever experienced in my young life. I was drawn to it in a way I could never quite describe or understand.

The Moki fort felt like wild Indians to me. Around every corner and in every nook and cranny, the essence of those ancient people lingered. They were always just beyond the range of my vision, but within the bounds of my knowing. I could feel them out there, watching from the shadows, and I was intrigued. I wanted to call out to them, to reach out and find them. Grandpa said they were dead and gone for centuries, but to me, they were very close. I could feel the warmth of their being in the touch of a broken pottery fragment, or a sliver of sparkling flint. The Anasazi, in their turn, reached out and touched my heart. I became a friend, a student, an ally and adopted son. I was never the same again after my first pilgrimage to that ruin.

We visited the fort several times when I was a little boy. Reed and I always went there with Uncle Nathan Noyes or with Grandpa. The fort stood more than 100 feet above the canyon floor on the very crest of a rocky summit. Grandma would not allow us to be up there by ourselves.

The ruin was a wonderland to me. Big chunks of painted pottery littered the hillside and slivers of multi-colored chert sparkled in the sun like broken shards of glass. Half-buried rock walls pushed up from the dirt. Squiggles, lines and little mountain sheep were etched into the desert varnish along the ledges.

She was an imposing structure, a massive stone box on the top of the hill. The ruin measured fifteen by twenty-two feet and stood twelve feet high. The fort had been two or three stories tall in antiquity, but the top floor may have been only a battlement. The fort was remarkably well preserved for having weathered the best Mother Nature could throw at her for at least seven hundred years.

The north-facing wall of the fort had long-ago collapsed, falling inward to the center of the building. Nothing remained of the roof beams or the willow and mud ceilings. They were dirt again, dissolved by rain and scattered by wind back to dust from whence they came. The building lay open and exposed to the elements, the sun peeking down into her secret, inner recesses where the once-proud north wall lay scattered.

White Canyon

There were lookout holes strategically placed in the walls at critical angles. Grandpa and Uncle Nate showed us the holes, and told us a man with a bow might actually be able to shoot through them. Reed and I took turns. One of us would look through the holes while positioning the other guy in the proper line of fire. We would then run over to see where the arrow might have landed so we could find the arrowhead. It was a good plan, but it never worked. We did find a couple of little arrow points during our excursions to the ruin, but we had to work hard for them. A lot of people had been there before us.

From the ruin we could look out across that river valley and see it all. The wide, muddy river, the cluttered little town, the airfield and Cass Hite's old house and farm across the river. It was a beautiful sight. The river valley was painted in red and brown with a sky as deep and blue as ocean waves.

The river was the dominating terrain feature in the valley, and she knew it. The Colorado was assertive, self-confident and proud. She smiled knowingly as she rolled past, slapping playfully at the ferryboat moored on its heavy cable against the far shore. The river was fat and happy and she flowed the way she had always flowed, free and wild and unrestricted. She was the queen of the canyon country and the very lifeblood of the desert, paying us little heed as she rolled on down the canyon. To Trachyte, past Red Canyon, then on to Ticaboo where Cass Hite lay sleeping.

The uranium mill was below us at the foot of the hill and toward the wash. We could watch little toy dump trucks scurrying about and hear the far-away metal clank of tailgates slamming shut as they dumped. The growling of the mill was far-off and filled the air with a distant rumble like a flash flood in the next canyon. The source of the sound was difficult to discern, like a jet plane passing high overhead above the clouds. Looking down at the mill, there seemed to be no reason for all the noise.

The boardinghouse and tarpaper cabins sat far below in their proper military regulation straight line. The asphalt roofing reflected some of the bright summer sunshine and the tops of the cabins glowed in the heat shimmer. The great sandstone ledge across the river was a towering mountain, its shadow staining the water along the edge of the river a dark and dusty gray.

Looking down from the ruin, the town was a bustling anthill of activity. Tiny little insect-people scurried about, unaware they were being watched from high on the hill. The mill hummed and the locusts buzzed. Sunshine sprinkled down from a royal blue sky. Cotton ball clouds cast moving shadows over the canyon floor. The big river smiled as she slid on past.

The Boardinghouse

Sometimes, on our way to or from the Indian ruin, we boys would stop to play on the tailings pile near the mill. The tailings pile was a great mound of purplish/gray dirt, the waste product of the uranium operation. In theory, all of the radioactive elements had been collected from the waste material. The pile sat next to the mill and near the main road. It was in the dooryard of the boardinghouse and we had to pass by it to get to or from the Indian fort.

The men were usually tolerant and would let us play on the tailings for a while before taking us back to the boardinghouse and Grandma. That big pile of soft dirt was irresistible to little boys. We would climb up on the pile and roll down the steep sides. It was hard to walk on the stuff because it had a very fine texture and we sank to the tops of our shoes. Reed and I would wrestle, toss handfuls of the colorful dust high in the air and play King of Bunker Hill. We would make snow-angels on top of the pile and go back to Grandma with the dander of the Atomic Monster in our clothes, shoes, hair and ears.

The men didn't think anything of us playing on the tailings pile because they worked at the mill everyday and handled the concentrated yellowcake without protective clothing or respirators. Company officials, engineers, and even government geologists, went about their business in the midst of the radioactive chemical wizardry without any safeguards or protective clothing. Some even laughed when a novice prospector drove past the tailings pile and got all excited when his Geiger counter buzzed so loud it almost jumped off the seat of his truck. We were all completely innocent. None of us suspected what the nuclear scientists already knew.

When the mill was dismantled in 1954, 26,000 tons of mill tailings were never relocated or buried. Lake Powell covered them in 1964. Most people who frequent the area today don't know there's a warm spot at the bottom of the lake that glows in the dark.[2]

In the early evening, the mill shut down for the day and the men were around. The feel and the attitude at the boardinghouse changed. Grandma wasn't in charge anymore. It was time for the men to talk and decide who would do what and when. The women became quieter and less assertive. They were always pleasant, sweet and cooperative, but the girls moved to the back of the bus.

When supper dishes were finished, Grandma would take us kids to the women's side of the bathhouse and give us a good scrubbing. Then we would all sit around outside where it was cool and listen and watch as the men laughed, joked and told stories, smoking cigarettes and drinking coffee and beer. People from the civilian side of town often came over to visit.

White Canyon

Everyone sat on chairs, boxes, or other improvised perches, up and away from the scorpions and spiders that came out in the dark. After bearing the heat of the day with their labors, the cool of the evening was a special treat and a time of rest.

My uncles didn't smoke or drink, and when I asked why, Grandma said it was because they were Mormons and they were special. Sometimes we Mormons drank soda pop while the other people drank coffee and beer. Grandma liked 7-up, but we boys liked Nesbitt orange. Grandma drank a lot of Nesbitt orange because that's what she kept in the refrigerator for the kids. Pop came in little seven-ounce glass bottles back then and it was a rare treat.

As the sun dipped behind the great rock wall across the river, a deep shadow spread across the valley. Mosquitoes sallied forth from among the willows and fat, happy frogs sang their little guts out in the gathering darkness. The day-shift locusts were tucked safely into bed and the dreaded blue-bellied lizards slunk away into the shadows. Tiny little bats zipped through the cottonwood trees, scooping up bugs and performing unbelievable feats of aerial acrobatics. A pale desert moon peeked over the hills far to the east. A red cast on the western horizon marked the sun's departure.

As the canyon grew dark, sounds became louder. Darkness seemed to amplify the slamming of a door or the loud laugh of a happy mill worker. The hum of the big diesel generator at the mill was more noticeable too. Sounds didn't travel like that in the sunlight. Sunlight absorbed sound, soaking it up and holding it back. The darkness deflected sound and the sounds bounced around in the shadows. The canyon echoed at night like a great, dark tunnel.

When the big diesel generator shut down at night, everything in the canyon stopped cold in the sudden stillness as the lights went out. People stopped talking as the wave of quiet darkness swept over them. Even frogs stopped singing in the river bottom and listened as the silence soaked into the night. And then, from somewhere nearby, a match would flare in the darkness as someone lit a coal-oil lamp. Then, the frogs and the talking would start up again, slowly. The talking was always softer in the dim light of the lamp. It was reserved and subdued, a reverent acquiescence to the stillness of the desert.

When the noise of the diesel generator went away and the canyon was dark, the desert crept in closer. Even the river came up closer in the dark. We knew it was closer because we could smell it closer. We could hear it closer too. We would lay in our warm beds in the darkness, and if we listened carefully … sometimes we could hear a splash out in the night, a log rolling over as the river carried it past, a beaver slapping his tail on the flat water, or a sandbank caving into the river.

The ledges moved closer in the darkness too. They stood taller and blocked out more of the sky than they did during the daytime. The ledges became flat and featureless shadows in the dark, an ominous presence looming high overhead that could be felt as well as seen.

Nighthawks came from out of the darkness and flashed through the sky like low-flying fighter jets, the raspy honk of their excited calls echoing down the canyon as they chased bugs in the moonlight. The moon grew strong in the darkening sky and shone bright like a polished silver dime. The sheen of polished silver cast shadows all along the sandstone wall across the river. Moon shadows moved slowly over the sandstone and the features of the ledges changed hour by hour. The river glistened in the night. It took on the appearance of ice or smooth cement, the contrast of its smoothness stark against the crags and folds of the canyon walls. The moon could see his handsome face reflected in the water, and he smiled smugly as he drifted lazily overhead.

From some vantage points, if a person looked hard, a single dim light could be seen across the river, just a little downstream. It was the flicker of a coal oil lamp at the Chaffin ferry landing, only a mile, but a world away.

Inside the cabin we snuggled next to Grandma on her big, soft bed and settled in for the night. The moonlight found its way into the room through the joints, cracks and nail holes in the walls like playful, silver sunbeams. Through the screen doors we could see the dark wall of ledges in the distance and the moon shadows creeping slowly across the desert floor. Nighthawks soared joyfully in the cool night air, polishing the bright face of the moon with their velvety wings. Frogs and happy crickets sang us to sleep.

Notes:

1. What the author calls locusts were probably Katydids. Everyone he knew as a boy called them locusts.

2. Energy Information Administration. www.eia.doe.gov . White Canyon Mill Site.

From the website:
The uranium mill at White Canyon processed 26,358 tons of ore between April 1949 and December 1953. 128,145 pounds of Uranium sodium diuranate

was sold to the Atomic Energy Commission during the life of the mill. On average, 43 percent of the ore's uranium was not recovered, but remained in the mill tailings impounded at the mill site. Based on the quantity of ore treated at the mill, the AEC estimated that some 26,000 tons of tailings were originally impounded at the mill site.

In November of 1963, when the future Lake Powell was scheduled to begin forming behind the Glen Canyon Dam, the AEC requested the Department of Health, Education and Welfare to determine what would be the future radiation effect of the White Canyon mill tailings, which contained an estimated 13 grams of radium-226, when flooded by the lake. The study concluded that, given the isolated location of the site and the dilution factor represented by the large volume of water in the lake, the mill tailings could remain at the former mill site and be inundated by the lake waters. It was postulated that, after a period of years, the natural action of sedimentation of the lake would cover the tailings under several feet of silt.

After the report was issued, the Vanadium Corporation of America removed some of the "high-grade" mill tailings and presumably shipped those tailings for reprocessing at their plant in Shiprock, New Mexico.

The former mill site and the old tailings pile were covered by the rising waters of Lake Powell in 1965. In October 1965, when the tailings were inundated, a series of water and bottom sediment samples were collected in the immediate vicinity of the tailings pile and also at intervals over a distance of several miles both upstream and downstream from the mill site. The old White Canyon mill tailings pile was determined to be covered with sediment distributed by the lake water. Further analysis of both the lake water and bottom sediment samples determined there was no significant variation in the levels of radioactivity between the samples collected upstream and downstream from the tailings site and from over the tailings site.

10
Uranium Pioneers

When the sun went behind the ledges on December 31, 1953, the uranium mill at White Canyon fell silent forever. It had fulfilled its destiny. The mill was shut down and the town began to die. People were expecting it. Everyone knew that the mill was a pilot project and its life was limited. Dump trucks filled with uranium ore were re-routed to mills at Monticello and Durango.

A few people, like Grandpa and Uncle Nate, were kept on the payroll to help dismantle the facilities. Most others were laid-off. Jeeps, trucks and camp trailers trickled out of the canyon like ragged gypsy caravans over a period of several weeks. Like the Anasazi, the desert dwellers were leaving and would never be back. Grandma ran the boardinghouse until the mill was dismantled and there was no one to cook for. That happened in July, 1954.

Living at the boardinghouse and tarpaper cabins in White Canyon Town had been roughing it enough, but when the mill closed my grandparents moved up the canyon a mile or more and made a homestead on clean desert sand. They lived there for another eighteen months. They were still deeply involved in the search for uranium and not ready to pack it in and move back to town yet. They were in their mid-50s and everything they owned had been invested in the search. To leave it all behind was a heartbreaking proposition. They resisted for as long as they possibly could.

The mill was gone, the town was gone, and almost all of the people were gone. The canyon was quiet and empty. Being left in semi-isolation in the middle of the desert was not a problem for Lorin and Bertha. They were right at home in the wilderness. They were only one generation removed from pioneers who had broken new ground all over the Mountain West. Their parents and grandparents had conquered the Utah wilderness. They had both been raised in log houses without electricity.

They saw the world differently than people see it today. Open, empty country was a land of opportunity to them. They were a living link to America's frontier experience and they understood it was the duty of civilized man to claim and tame the wilderness. Brigham Young had taught their fathers that it was man's sacred responsibility to make wilderness a place for peaceful habitation. Men were to wrestle from the earth the treasures that Almighty God had placed there for those bold enough to claim them.

White Canyon

Fertile soil, minerals, oil, water, timber and grass, were God's gift to men. A man was foolish if he didn't accept those gifts and make full use of them.

The Foster family leaving White Canyon after the uranium mill was closed. Jeanie, Elaine and "Charlie the dog" on the truck. LaVon and Nephi Foster with Elmer Johnson the ferryboat operator, standing in front of the truck.
Photo courtesy of Jeanie Foster McDoniel

Uranium Pioneers

John Lorin (J.L.) and Bertha Wardle Winn were rooted in that other century, and they were amazing people. They were from Utah's Uintah Basin, the Ute Indian Reservation at the foot of the Uintah Mountains. They grew up in Vernal, White Rocks and Fort Duchesne. Both were the offspring of tried and true, wilderness tempered, blue-blood Mormon pioneer stock. Log cabins and wilderness homesteads were a part of their memories, as well as their heritage. Her grandfather, George Wardle, was with the first pioneer company to enter the Salt Lake valley with Brigham young on July 24, 1847. His grandfather, Dennis Alma Winn, was born in Salt Lake City in December 1849 when the city of Zion was only two years old.

Lorin and Bertha Winn - 1967

She was born in 1898. He in 1900. They were married in 1919 when he was eighteen and she was almost twenty-one. Like their parents and grandparents before them, they sought new ground and new opportunities as they began a life together. They left the Uintah Basin forever and migrated to Castle Valley (Carbon County, Utah). He got a job as a blacksmith, shoeing horses and mules at the coalmine in Sunnyside.

He was a good-looking man with a dark complexion and the muscles of a blacksmith. He reminded me in many ways of Clark Gable, the movie star.

White Canyon

He was a man's man, rough and coarse in many ways, fond of strong drink and a good game of pool now and then. He had rowdy friends and he was the undisputed master of his own home. He chain-smoked cigarettes, and rolled his own the way most of the old-timers did. Bull Durham and Prince Albert were his friends. He rolled cuffs into his pant legs and often used the cuffs as ashtrays when he smoked inside the house, a crude, log cabin trait that sometimes drove the womenfolk to despair. He was prone to anger, even violence at times, and was a key participant in a rowdy barroom brawl that almost got him thrown in jail when he was sixty years old.

In spite of all that, he was a good grandpa. He had a wry sense of humor and he was a great tease. He made up silly little poems and would recite them with a wide grin and a twinkle in his eye. He was surprisingly tolerant of clumsy little boys and ever willing to take us along with him on his many adventures. He taught us to fish. He loved to fly-fish and I've never met his equal on a trout stream. He was a master of the art. He would sometimes take his old bamboo fly rod and practice casting out on the lawn in front of his home in Wellington. He would make long and graceful casts and snatch bottle caps from the grass with the fishhook.

He was not well educated, but he loved to read and he was self-taught in a variety of interesting subjects. He knew history, geography and geology. He could give a complete dissertation on the battle of Waterloo, the Morrison geologic formation, or the political and economic situation in Eastern Europe. Winston Churchill was his hero. He was interested in Western American history and he knew it well. He was a prospector at heart and always had his rock hammer and canvas sample bags behind the seat of his old pickup truck. He kept a loaded pistol under the seat.

He was imaginative and inventive, a Tinker who could fix anything. He worked at the coalmines for years and then opened a small automotive garage in Wellington. He was a good mechanic, welder, blacksmith and jack-of-all-trades. He made his living with his hands and he was good at what he did.

He was a free spirit, apt to bend the rules now and then and color outside the lines. One of the first memories I have of him was when he had me sitting on a bar stool, drinking orange soda pop while he drank beer. I was three or four years old. He was smoking, drinking, playing pool and laughing with the guys. His brother Ralph, my great-uncle, was tending bar. I'll never forget the tart smell of the place, stale beer and cigarette smoke, or how dark it was in there. The bright neon signs, and especially the mirrors behind the bar, fascinated me. In the mirrors, it was like everything was happening twice. The scene of the crime was the old Savoy Bar in Price, and mother would have killed him if only she had known. I was his first grandchild and he proudly introduced me to every drunk and barroom floozy in the place and taught me to shake their hands.

Grandma, on the other hand, was a saint. She was deeply religious and always went to church. True to her Mormon heritage and upbringing, she neither smoked nor drank alcohol or coffee. She did tolerate those things in her husband; however, and he always had a pot of coffee on the stove and a half-filled ashtray on the kitchen table.

Bertha was a woman born in the nineteenth century who knew her place around her man. She deferred to him in all things, following him dutifully and obediently. She was also completely dependent upon him. She never learned to drive a car, and except for those few years at the boardinghouse, she never worked outside the home. He took care of the money, the bills, and all expenditures. Her job was to take care of the house and raise the kids.

The two of them recognized a division of the sexes that was quaint by today's standards and a legacy of their pioneer upbringing. Men and women were different and they didn't do things together. When visiting their home, they would be sure the men all retired to one room to talk "man talk," while the women stayed in another room to talk "woman talk." Little boys went with the women until they were eight or ten, and then they could sit with the men if they were quiet and respectful. If young boys got fidgety, rowdy, or out-of-hand, they were sent back to the women for a while - in disgrace.

In their world, men didn't cook, wash clothes or change diapers. Women didn't work outside of the home. Women wore skirts and aprons. Men wore Levis and boots. Women wore their hair long. Men kept their hair cut short. Women wore earrings and men wore hats. Women taught little girls to cook and sew. Men taught little boys to hunt, fish, and fix cars. Men went away to war or to work in the coalmines. Women stayed home with the babies and prayed for them. Men opened doors for women. The women smiled graciously and said "Thank you." It was all so simple, and the world went round and round.

Grandma was a woman tempered by hard work and sore trials. She knew the world for what it was, but she kept herself apart from it. She was ever true to her ideals and her religious heritage. There was deep kindness in her smile and her eyes always shone with love, hope, and understanding. She glowed with the radiance of faith, and she was always clean, neat and gracious. She was outgoing, charitable and ever willing to sacrifice herself for the good of others. She knew the pain of longsuffering and the agony of unfulfilled dreams, and that helped to make her very compassionate. In her whole life she never had a formal portrait made, and my heart bleeds.

And yet, in spite of her longsuffering, selflessness and faithful acquiescence toward her husband, she was a strong woman. At her core she was rock-solid, firm and uncompromising, ever true to her convictions. She was surprisingly tolerant towards others, but we all knew there was a point where she would draw the line and stand and fight. She never allowed her principles to be compromised.

She seldom laughed out loud, but she often smiled. She had a haunting smile, bright and honest, but deep, knowing, and thoughtful too. She was always serious and I never heard her tell a joke. And yet, there was a spark of humor in her that would show up occasionally.

She was a skilled practitioner of folk medicine and she always treated our colds, sore throats and other childhood illnesses with hot chicken soup, poultices, mustard plasters, oven-heated flannel and Ben-Gay. She spoke of the horrors of the great flu epidemic of 1918, and once said the thing she feared more than anything else was a baby's cough in the night. She had buried her first child as an infant.

Her instinct for when and how to treat illness, especially in children, was uncanny. And while her methods were often unconventional, her cures were real. She knew that the best painkiller was hugs, kisses and warm feet, and she freely made that diagnosis and dispensed that medicine. She and mother made us kids choke down a sip of cod-liver-oil in the mornings to strengthen our blood, and Grandma often drank a bitter, homemade Mormon pioneer health tonic called Brigham Tea (boiled mountain rush stems).

In the fall, she canned anything she could get into a quart bottle and a pressure cooker. She made full and absolute use of the vegetable garden and bought bushels of apples, pears and apricots from others. She made bread every week. She loved homemade bread and potato soup with onions - hardy staples from her pioneer past. She made raisin bread as a treat and always had a loaf on hand.

She loved kids, and she would read to us at night and tell us stories. She was generous with smiles and hugs. She told us about God and heaven, taught us to pray and encouraged us to go to church. She was the best grandmother in the whole world and I snuggled to her bosom as a child. Her love and warmth enveloped me completely. I loved her dearly.

As she got older, she suffered from an ailment known as Bright's disease. Bright's disease is an inflammation of the kidneys. None of us made the connection at the time, and if her doctor knew he never said, but Bright's disease is an early indicator of radiation poisoning. She might have acquired the disease while working at the boardinghouse in the shadow of the big uranium tailings pile from the mill.

Lorin and Bertha grew up in a world without indoor plumbing and electricity, and they could do just fine without those things. They were content in a log cabin or a tent with a coal oil lamp and an outhouse on the edge of the timber, and they lived like that often. They ran a sawmill in Joe's Valley for a few years and lived in a remote cabin on the mountain. They also ran the pump house in Range Creek for the city of Sunnyside for a year or two and lived in almost total isolation in a deep mountain canyon. The pumps pushed fresh water over Patmos Mountain to the town of Sunnyside. They were snowed-in during the winter and came to town only a few times during the summer.

Surprisingly, it was often Grandma who encouraged the moves to the wilderness. She truly loved the desert and the mountains, but I think one of the reasons she was happiest in the outback was because she had her man all to herself. She could tame him in the wilderness. She could keep him away from his rowdy friends, the bars and strong drink. He needed her on the desert. He was her friend, companion and confidant. He wasn't always as close or as compassionate when they lived closer to town.

They never seemed to be madly in love, my grandparents. The few times I did see them hold hands or kiss one another they seemed to be awkward and embarrassed about it. But then, they came from a time when such open displays of affection were frowned upon. Their marriage was more a partnership and a working relationship than a Romeo and Juliet romance. They were both loyal to the partnership; however, and they were married for fifty-seven years, until his death in 1976. She followed him to heaven two years later, when her broken heart stopped to rest.

Together they were an unbeatable team. They were focused, willing to sacrifice, and they could get by on almost nothing. They were a pair of bold adventurists, never afraid to take a chance or accept the challenge of a new job or new opportunity. That's how they came to be in White Canyon.

The uranium boom of the early fifties was exciting, filled with opportunity and irresistible to people like them. Like true forty-niners (1949 this time), they pulled up stakes and migrated to the red desert and the heart of the action. They were part of that hard-core of bold, dream-chasing opportunists, willing to take a chance and start all over again in their early fifties. They were true pioneers.

White Canyon

When word got around in the late 1940s that the government was paying big money for uranium, Lorin Winn was one of the first to start spending every weekend on the desert with a rock hammer in his hand. It was suspected there were commercial-grade deposits of radioactive treasure out near Hanksville somewhere, but no one had found the Mother Lode yet.

Grandpa gave it his best shot and he actually found a little high-grade. He staked some claims on the San Rafael Reef and sold a few loads of good ore. Unfortunately, the deposit was very shallow and soon petered out. He was disappointed of course, but that first small success fed the fires of his ambition.

Temple Mountain - 1951
Left to right - Reon McCourt, Tom McCourt, Bertha Winn,
Reed McCourt, Lorin Winn. Winn family photo

With a partner, Danny Collins, Lorin contracted to develop some uranium properties in the Temple Mountain area that were owned by other men. For years, vanadium had been mined at Temple Mountain and uranium had been an unwanted byproduct that piled up as waste around the entrances of the mines. In the 1940s, Temple Mountain was one of the first areas in the United States to make a contribution to the strategic reserve of domestic Uranium, and much of it came from those vanadium discard piles.

Between 1949 and 1951, Lorin Winn and Dan Collins worked the Temple Mountain properties. Two of grandpa's young sons, Var and Jack, worked with them. The boys drove ore trucks from Temple Mountain to the nearest ore-processing mill in Monticello, Utah, about 160 miles away. Much of the distance was on primitive roads and it took all day to make a round-trip.

Grandpa was ready and willing to track the Atomic Monster down, but he needed some backing. He was a man of humble means and prospecting for a living doesn't pay well until you find the pot of gold. He just didn't have the money or the recourses to sail out on the desert and stay there. He needed a grubstake. At the beginning of 1952, he got his big chance. It was the fulfillment of his dreams and an answer to Grandma's prayers. A chance to live on the desert full-time and find radioactive treasure. Bertha helped him out when she won the contract to manage the boardinghouse and feed the mill workers at White Canyon. It was the first and only job she ever had. Grandpa signed on to work at the mill and it became a joint venture. Their two handsome young sons, Var and Jack, and a son-in-law, Nathan Noyes, all signed on to be mill workers too. It became a grand and exciting family adventure.

Actually, it was Nathan Noyes who broke ground and prepared the way for the rest of them. Uncle Nate was a native son of Hanksville, and he grew up with sand in his shoes. He had worked at the White Canyon mill and lived in the cabin-billets for a year before marrying Aunt Lorraine in 1951. He's the one who spread the word that they were looking for a matron to run the boardinghouse and there were good jobs waiting for the men at the uranium mill. Uncle Nate was the scout, trailbreaker and wagon boss who rounded up the rest of them and guided them on that pioneering journey to The Promised Land. Actually, he once said that what really happened was the whole family followed him to White Canyon because he stole the baby when he married 17-year-old Aunt Lorraine.

The jobs with the Vanadium Corporation gave Lorin and Bertha a good steady income, and they were living right smack in the middle of the best uranium hunting grounds in the world. Every weekend, and nights after work, the sound of grandpa's rock hammer echoed in the canyons. The big strike was always just a little higher up the hill, or just a little further down the canyon. He was on top of the world as he followed radioactive monster tracks into the ledges. Move over Charlie Steen, here I come.

I was always proud of my Aunts and Uncles. They are good, descent and honest people. My uncles were my heroes when I was a kid. They were strong and handsome young men. They swaggered around town in their tin hardhats and they often went without shirts in the sweltering heat, muscles rippling beneath the suntans. They were young men accustomed to hard work and responsibility. They radiated health, strength and energy. They were proud atomic warriors and they did their part for flag and country by sacking the monster so other men could stuff him into bomb casings. They always walked tall and I wanted to grow up to be just like them.

Uncle Jack was an athlete, muscled and bronze, the intrepid young stallion of the family. I used to hide from him because he would throw me high in the air over his head and then catch me on the way down. He would laugh and laugh, but it would scare me so bad I would almost wet myself. He played football as a young man and he was always active, laughing and full of fun. He loved practical jokes and he kept people on their toes.

His wife, Aunt Melba, was pretty: golden hair, a bright smile, and graceful as a cat. She was also smart, practical and hard working. She was never afraid to speak her mind and I always admired that quality in her. She was a strong young woman and always involved and ready to serve. She loved to laugh and she was always on the go. Sometimes Uncle Jack had to tread smartly to keep up.

Var was tall, dark and quiet. He was big and strong and he wore a hearing aid. He didn't marry until he was in his thirties. The years he lived in White Canyon he was a bachelor. He was an introvert and buried himself in hobbies. He tied fishing flies like no one else could. He would sit for hours amid piles of silk floss and feathers, and tie some of the most beautiful hand-tied flies anywhere. He was a religious stalwart of the little community and he walked the straight and narrow in everything he did.

Uncle Nathan Noyes grew up in Hanksville and he was right at home on the desert. He was a fine young man, one of the best the world has ever produced. He exemplified every Boy Scout virtue. He was soft-spoken and almost shy, a good-looking young man with a ready smile and deep, thoughtful eyes. He was thin but surprisingly strong. He surprised everyone by winning a five-dollar bet that he could lift a 350 pound cask of yellowcake onto the back of a truck by himself. He was deeply religious, a devout Mormon Elder, and he went to church every Sunday. He and Aunt Lorraine were madly in love, and still just kids.

Nathan and Lorraine Noyes

Var Winn

White Canyon

Nate and Lorraine lived in a tiny camp trailer on the civilian side of White Canyon Town for a few months before the rest of the family signed on. Later they would build a twelve by twenty-four foot tarpaper house and let Myron Ferre rent the trailer to someone else.

Uncle Jack and Aunt Melba lived in a tent-house for the first few months they were on the desert and rented the place from Myron Ferre. Tent-houses were common in White Canyon. They were built with wooden floors and low sub-walls, but with a tent forming the roof. It was a lot like living in a big covered wagon without wheels. Jack and Melba shared the tent-house with two baby daughters and a tribe of healthy desert crickets. The bugs loved the place and could not be exorcised from it. The crickets slept in the cool shade of airy canvas during the day, and put on marvelous concerts during the night.

Reed and I never lived with our grandparents full-time, but stayed with them often, sometimes for weeks. We loved White Canyon and we loved to be at Grandma's house. We pestered our parents continuously to let us go and stay for a few days. Grandma always seemed happy to have us around, even though she was very busy, and the pickup and delivery of little boys was not too complicated. Family members beat the road between Price and White Canyon to powder hauling truckloads of groceries to the boardinghouse. And besides, aunt Lorraine tried to kidnap us every chance she got. She didn't have any kids of her own yet, and to her, taking little boys on the desert was like playing with a box of puppies.

The family lived in White Canyon Town from the very beginning of 1952 until the last of the town's people were gone in the summer of 1954. Then, my grandparents and Uncle Jack and his family stayed even longer. Grandpa and Jack were both involved in other uranium mining ventures and they hadn't found El Dorado yet.

Some months before the mill was shut down, Jack quit his job there and went to work for the Smith Mining and Exploration Company based in Houston Texas. Smith Mining was one of dozens of companies migrating to Utah to invest in the search for uranium. Jack was twenty-five years old but a young man of ability. The Smith brothers hired him to run their Utah operations for them.

Jack was determined to find the Atomic Monster for his new employers and he boldly led the charge. His little band of atomic scouts and uranium warriors chased the Monster all across the desert, but with limited success. They found Monster tracks, scat, and old nests, but the Monster wasn't there anymore. They found just enough atomic dander to tease the Geiger counter and sucker them into drilling deep, but the glory holes had all been found by then. They were a year or two too late.

Jack and Melba Winn

Jack ran the Smith Mining operation for a little more than two years. Then, at the beginning of 1956, Smith Mining decided to cut their losses and move to greener pastures. Jack had won the respect of company owners and he was invited to move his family to Houston where the Smith Company was headquartered. They were there for many years.

When the mill was gone, Uncle Nate was one of the few men who continued to work for the Vanadium Corporation. But without the mill, he and Lorraine had to move to Durango. By then, Uncle Var was in Oakland, California serving a mission for the LDS church.

When the last of the company people left White Canyon in July 1954, Lorin and Bertha were both laid-off and lost their grubstake. When that happened, he went to work for his son Jack at Smith Mining. Lorin and Bertha put together a homestead up the canyon and hung on until 1956.

Grandpa had been in the uranium finding business since 1949, and even though he had a full-time job at the mill, he had prospected and filed claims and helped to organize his own mining company. With a partner, George Wofford, he incorporated the Southern Cross Uranium Company in 1953. Doctor J. Eldon Dorman joined the company in early 1954 and became a key partner. The Southern Cross was one of hundreds of partnerships incorporated in the early fifties to find and mine uranium. A man on his own with a Geiger counter could sometimes find the stuff, but a man on his own could seldom mine and market it. Some have said that finding uranium was actually the easy part. The greater challenge was securing capital to develop the properties. Then as now, it takes money to make money. The pooling of resources into small partnership companies was a way for the little fish to swim with the sharks.

Grandpa was a working partner in the Southern Cross venture and he gave it everything he had. He chased the radioactive rainbow all over the desert with a jeep and a Geiger counter. On behalf of the Southern Cross Company, he filed several mining claims in the Hite, White Canyon, and Red Canyon areas, and they held some potentially valuable properties in North Wash. It was an adventure and they almost made some money. They thought they were rich more than once, but it never happened.

The Southern Cross partners still held legal claims and were negotiating to secure financial backing to develop the properties when congress authorized Lake Powell in 1956. The lake and the proposed Canyonlands National Park would drown or cut access to most of their holdings. The Southern Cross partners went to court but received no recompense for the property, investments, or the years of hard work and effort. Like Arth Chaffin, the government Goliath trampled the deeds to their mining claims underfoot.

Somewhere on those rocky heights above Lake Powell, and tucked safely into the enfolding arms of Canyonlands National Park, there are still some irreverent little rock cairns with duly notarized legal papers that give Lorin Winn and the Southern Cross Uranium Company exclusive rights to the minerals. [1]

Notes:

1. In 2004 the author found one of those uranium claim markers filed by his grandfather on behalf of the Southern Cross Uranium Company. The document was in a rusted Prince Albert tobacco tin buried in a rock cairn in North Wash. The signatures of all three shareholders of the company were on the document: Lorin Winn, J. Eldon Dorman and George Wofford. The name of the claim was Small Water #3 and the claim was filed on May 28, 1954. The document was weathered and tattered, but still legible after 50 years exposed to the elements.

Southern Cross Uranium Company claim marker in North Wash. The tobacco can on the rock, containing the official claim registration papers, was recovered from the rock cairn.
Author photo - February 2004

White Canyon

11
The Road To White Canyon

For me, a lot of what I remember best about the red desert of my childhood was experienced during those trips to and from White Canyon. It took several hours to make the journey from our home in Wellington and the pilgrimage covered the whole spectrum of the desert country, from the barren clay hills at the foot of the Book Cliffs near Green River, to the deep red sand and towering stone monuments of the Colorado River canyon. It is the most beautiful country in the world and I still love to travel through it.

Back then, before Interstate 70, a dirt road turned off Highway 6 and bumped out into the boondocks a few miles west of the town of Green River. The road headed south to where the Henry Mountains could be seen peeking over the horizon. A state road sign pointed down the dusty track and announced that Hanksville, the Hite Ferry, and White Canyon Town were somewhere out that-a-way. The road crossed a desert wash and climbed a series of long, barren and gray-colored hills. On the backside of the hills the desert was waiting. From that vantage the road disappeared into the heat shimmer far to the south. It was the early 1950s and there was not a plume of dust out there anywhere to suggest that another traveler might want to share the road.

The country was open and empty for as far as we could see, a home for coyotes, ravens and range cows. To the right stood the San Rafael Reef, a magnificent wall of broken sandstone that juts up suddenly from the desert floor and claws at the sky with fingers of stone that are many hundreds of feet tall. The vertical wall of rock extends to the south for fifty miles, slowly petering out and veering to the right as it gets closer to Hanksville.

To the left of the road the country is mostly sand hills with little tabletop mesas adding variety, texture and depth to the yellow sand and sagebrush. Far to the east, a hazy image of the La Sal Mountains hangs suspended on the horizon as if cast on the sky by a movie projector. The base of the mountain is completely lost in the heat shimmer, and the mountain appears to float on the horizon like a cloud. The entire image is faded and pale, filtered by too many miles of desert haze.

The road crossed the San Rafael River on a rickety little bridge that deposited the traveler almost in the dooryard of the Hatt ranch, a desert oasis of cottonwood trees and green pastures with a small house and stock corrals. After leaving Hatt's ranch, the road topped a long sandy ridge, then plunged down into the sand bumps and Brigham tea bushes toward Hanksville, some forty miles away. The road was full of sandpits, washboards and oversized gravel nodules. Progress was slow and painful.

There was a rickety store and service station at a place called Temple Junction. It was where the road to Hanksville forked with one branch going west toward Temple Mountain and Goblin Valley. A few dented-up pickup trucks and scruffy old prospectors were sometimes lounging around in front of the place, smoking and drinking beer. A mile or so on the right, down the Temple Mountain road toward Goblin Valley, was a tall wooden windmill and some rough-cut plank corrals. The windmill stood as a sentinel over a little sand flat valley, a monument to man's ingenuity and a rest stop for wing-weary raptors in that land with no trees.

Back on the road to Hanksville, there were no fences following the road in those days. The desert was unrestrained. She stretched endless and free to all horizons. Sand and rabbit brush squeezed tight against the dirt road as if trying to reclaim it. Sometimes people got stuck in the sand. If it rained or snowed, a person might get stuck in mud instead of sand. It was always a good idea to carry a shovel, tow chain, bumper jack (called a sheepherder jack, back then) and a set of tire chains, just in case.

San Rafael Reef north of Hanksville
Author photo

The Road To White Canyon

There were no road signs on that caravan trail and the road set it's own speed limits. The ruts and washboards would jar a person's teeth loose if he tried to go fast, and every wash and gully offered the possibility of a bog hole, flash flood, or a two foot drop-off where the road had been washed out from the previous flash flood. Travelers sometimes had to take up shovels and donate an hour of free labor to the Utah highway department just to get through.

We often took the road at night. It was cooler then, and in those days before automotive air-conditioning, much more comfortable. The night trips were always exciting adventures to me. Out on the vastness of the desert the night sky was a wonder to behold. To look out at that endless panorama of glistening stars was like being in the Starship Enterprise. Beam me up Scottie, and warp speed into eternity. It was truly spectacular. My imagination always went into hyper-drive.

Out across the sand flats, rock spires cast long shadows in the moonlight, and the snow-capped tips of the Henry Mountains shone brightly in the night sky. The long, dark shadow of the San Rafael Reef loomed tall and rigid to the west, while sand dunes rippled like ocean waves across the flats. The sandstone reef became the Barbary Coast at night, a rocky shore for the desert to splashed up against in the weak moonlight.

The desert had a different feel in the night. Everything was turned upside down. In the daylight, it was the land that held your attention. The rock formations, sand bumps and distant mountains. In the night, it was the sky that became the focus as the earth went dark. Your eyes, thoughts and consciousness were pulled upward as the night sky came alive. From endless depths the desert sky reached out and touched my heart in ways the red sand never did. The deep and vast emptiness of the diamond-chipped heavens brought God and eternity much closer. To look into eternity made me pull my thoughts and feelings deep inside myself.

Traveling anywhere on the desert at night in those days was like setting out on a vast, dark ocean. The shadowy sage-covered hills were great black waves in an endless sea of sand. Across the waves, one seldom saw the lights of another ship. A dark horizon stretched far into the night, to wherever that cellophane sheet of stars in the night sky ended. Sometimes the stars seemed light-years away, and sometimes as close as the windshield of the truck. The stars were polished bright by the soft velvet of the desert night, sparkling and glistening in the moonlight.

Out on that dark ocean of sand, there were no towns, signposts or distant lights to guide by. Only that thin line of rough and dusty road. The road was a lifeline, the single connecting thread that tied civilization to civilization across the vastness of the outback. And at night, the road stretched into empty darkness. To follow it was an exercise in faith.

On a moonless night, the road disappeared at the end of the headlights. Beyond the reach of that weak beam the desert was dark and wild again. The little truck bumped along slowly, the headlights probing the road ahead, feeling for obstacles, plumbing the depths, revealing rocks and bushes, lighting up puddles.

I marveled at how the whole world was gray and black in the night shadows until touched by the weak beam of the headlights. Then, how colors instantly came to life when touched by the light. Gray cottonwood leaves magically turned dusty green in the weak light. Black sand bumps and rocks blushed red and brown. Then, as the headlights passed them by, the colors quickly went to black and gray again. It was magic.

I remember the excitement when a jackrabbit or a mouse would be captured in the headlights for a fleeting moment. The stunned creature would be confused and acting silly, his dignity and proper wild-animal decorum compromised by the unexpected appearance of the bright-eyed pickup truck bearing down on him in the night. We boys squealed with delight when a Kangaroo rat jumped excitedly up and down like he was on a pogo-stick, or when a stupid Jackrabbit tried to evade us by running straight away and down the road, finally dodging quickly to the side and throwing a splash of sand high in the air as he dove for cover. Even Grandpa would laugh.

And sometimes, far out ahead, the headlights would catch the sparkle of wild eyes in the night: a fox, coyote, or bobcat. The light in those eyes would burn bright for only a moment, then disappear into the dark again. Those burning eyes were sobering reminders of the wildness of the desert. Out there somewhere in the night were evil, predatory and shadowy creatures. They were living and breathing ghouls with sharp teeth and claws that stalked the sand and killed things in the starlight. From deep in the darkness, those wild and burning eyes made little boys feel very small and vulnerable.

I was very much aware that we were alone on that ocean of sand, and at the mercy of the desert and the mechanical reliability of that little pickup truck. But at the same time, I knew my grandpa was a blacksmith, a mechanic, and a good Captain to sail with. He had tools and skills and even a gun. He was big, strong and brave. He would take care of me.

In such a remote and isolated place, we didn't often see other travelers, especially at night. Sometimes from a high place we would see a faint, distant light from another vehicle, many miles off, on Highway 6 or

Highway191. Those distant, flickering spots of light would shimmer and struggle on the horizon for a few seconds and then disappear forever back into the blackness. They were like phantoms, faraway little sparks of life, fleeting and noiseless reminders that other people were out there somewhere on that ocean of darkness.

Sometimes it was a shock to see just how far away that other person was. I could feel the distance to those tiny dots of light as if a great void had opened up across the desert. Between us was only black emptiness. Those tiny lights were as far away and as out of touch as the distant winking light of a satellite passing high overhead among the stars. The realization was sobering and the sense of isolation overwhelming. The desert was empty. There was no way to communicate with anyone. A distress signal or a cry for help would be wasted on the burrowing owls and the uncaring kit foxes.

Grandpa's truck didn't have a radio, and sometimes we traveled for miles and miles in the night without anyone speaking. We would sit quietly and look out the windows and watch as the dark waves of the desert flowed slowly past, all thoughts and feelings turned inward.

Inside the pickup truck it was very dark but for the faint glow of the instrument panel. Grandpa chain-smoked Bull Durham cigarettes, and when I think of those night trips, I always remember the sweet, pungent smell of that hand-rolled tobacco and the glow of his cigarette in the dark cab of the truck. He would steer the truck with his elbows while rolling another cigarette, and then steer with one hand while he stuffed his Bull Durham pouch back into this shirt pocket. He would light the smoke with a wooden kitchen match, and the stink of sulfur in that confined space would slam my nose shut and my eyes would water. And then, the sweet incense of tobacco would chase the sulfur stink away.

Grandpa would strike the match against his pant leg. He would raise his right leg slightly, there on the truck seat, to pull the denim of his Levis tight, then rip the match across his thigh. The match would burst into flame with a hiss and a bright yellow flash of light. I practiced and practiced lighting a match that way when I was a kid, and eventually mastered the trick. I also learned to do it another way Grandpa sometimes did it, and that was to pop a match to life with a thumbnail while holding it in the same hand. Grandpa knew a lot of neat little Humphrey Bogart tricks like that.

As we approached Hanksville, there were two river bridges to cross, one over the Muddy, the other over the Fremont River. They were quite close together, about a quarter of a mile apart. The two rivers joined a short distance below the bridges and together they became the Dirty Devil River.

White Canyon

As we approached the river bridges in the dark, we could see the flat surface of the water shining in the night. The rivers twisted through the darkness and glowed in the moonlight like molten silver. The old bridges were rickety, one-lane affairs with plank superstructures. As a car passed over them they would make loud noises like horses galloping on a hardwood floor. As we crossed the bridges, Grandpa would always yell, "Watch out! Here come the Indians!" And of course, every time, we boys would jump up and look out the back window of the truck to see. Our grandparents would laugh and laugh and Reed and I would be embarrassed. We fell for it every time, even when we knew it was coming. We just couldn't help ourselves.

And then, quite suddenly, we were in the middle of Hanksville. On a dark night the town would sneak up on you. We crossed the bridges and the road continued on as it had for many miles. But suddenly there was a dim light in the darkness framed by curtains. Framed by curtains? Yes. Framed by curtains. We were passing through the middle of town.

Hanksville in those days lacked asphalt, electricity and indoor plumbing. Technologically she was still in the dark ages, just like White Canyon. If not for seeing that coal oil lamp through a window, it was possible to pass through town on a dark night and not even know it. But then of course, there were usually other markers. The barking of a dog, the sudden appearance of a white picket fence, or an old milk cow standing by the side of the road in the headlights.

The town was wrapped and packaged in darkness, and of course, there was no chance to buy coffee, a hamburger or a gallon of gas. Hanksville went dark when the sun went down and everyone went to bed with the chickens.

Our passing in the night disturbed the slumber of the little place. The townspeople were not accustomed to traffic on the night road. Shadowy faces would peek through dimly lit windows. A door would open and a dark figure would step out on a porch to cuss or reward an excited dog. Sometimes the beam of a flashlight would follow us down the road and chase us out of town. Driving through town didn't take long on a dark night. Soon we were out on the desert again.

From Hanksville, the old road continued south toward the Henry Mountains. It went 10 or 12 miles to the Fairview Ranch, then veered east around the foot of the Henry Mountains before dropping down into North Wash. The new road, highway 95, lacks the charm and the tickle hills of the old road. The new highway is aimed more to the southeast as it leaves town, straight as an arrow, wide and hard surfaced with painted yellow lines, culverts and guardrails. A no-nonsense thoroughfare of commerce and tourism. An unseeing, unfeeling, get-there-and-be-gone, 80 miles-an-hour pipeline to somewhere else.

For me, I like the convenience of the new road, but I miss the charm and the communion with the desert of the old road. At 30 miles-per-hour you could feel the tickle hills, roll your window down, smell the sage brush and get dirt in your ears. The old road made the desert more personal.

In North Wash, the old road bumped, twisted and crossed the wash more than thirty times before finally breaking free from the confining stone walls to find the Colorado River. We always strained hard to catch that first glimpse of the river. It was always so exciting to see that huge expanse of moving water after crossing almost two hundred miles of desert.

North Wash emptied into the Colorado about five miles north of the Hite Ferry. At the point of confluence the road turned south to follow the river. I remember that stretch of road best in the daylight. A person didn't get the full impact of it in the dark.

The road between North Wash and Hite was bulldozed along a narrow strip of land that was sandwiched between the river and a massive sandstone wall. The wall towered hundreds of feet overhead. Going south to Hite, the river was on your left and the sandstone wall on your right, and it was a tight fit. In a couple of places there was just enough room for the road. It was always a little disconcerting to look out the truck window and see nothing but deep water on one side and a solid rock wall on the other. A person could get claustrophobic squeezed in like that.

While traveling that narrow road, we could not see the top of the rock wall above us. The ledge hung heavy over the road, several hundred feet high. Its shadow darkened the river in the afternoons, making the ledge seem even more ominous. Massive sandstone slabs had fallen from high above over the years and the road twisted through those barriers. Some of the rocks were as large as houses and shattered into huge stone splinters from the impact.

It was always cool and shady against the big ledge, but the shadow only increased the tension as the little truck squeezed through the rocky debris that had fallen for centuries. The shade was more like a portent of evil than a welcomed relief from the summer sun.

Tamarack bushes grew thick along that well-watered and narrow strip of earth. They reached out and clawed at the truck as it passed by. Stiff wooden fingers scraped along rigid metal skin and left wavy claw marks in the dust on the paint. The claws made screeching, screaming sounds like fingernails on a chalkboard that sent shivers down my spine.

In the springtime, all along that river road, the musty smell of tamarack blossoms was overpowering. The confining ledge and the hot, damp air of the river held the pollinated dust suspended near the ground to be stirred by the passing truck. The air was sometimes so thick with the warm dusty-smelling pollen that it was hard to breathe. Everyone coughed, and sometimes we put handkerchiefs over our mouth and noses. My eyes always felt gritty for a long time after traveling through the river bushes. Sometimes when a thin shaft of sunlight broke through the dark shadow of the overhanging ledge, clouds of pollen could be seen floating in the air like gold dust in the sunbeams.

Across the river the sun shone brightly against the red hills where Grandma's house waited. I always wished I could be over there. The red hills looked warm and friendly and a person could breathe over there. Across the river there were no big rocks hanging overhead, choking clouds of pollen dust, or the muddy fingers of the river reaching for the road.

Grandma was always apprehensive and fretful when traveling the road under the big ledge. She seemed to have her head pulled down deep into her shoulders and she held her breath a lot. She seemed to focus on the dashboard of the truck, not the deep water or the towering rock wall. Sometimes she fidgeted nervously with her fingers.

Sometimes there were rocks in the road, softball, basketball, and even beach ball sized rocks. Many of them punched several inches deep into the surface of the dirt road after free falling a few hundred yards through the stratosphere. Grandpa would stop the truck and get out to move them and Grandma would fret, wringing her hands and telling him to hurry up. He always ignored her, and sometimes smiled at her impatience. But sometimes he would get out of the truck and stand cautiously for a few moments looking up. He was tracing the path the rock had fallen, checking to be safe before putting himself in harm's way.

It was always refreshing to finally break free from the gloomy shadow of the big ledge and drive out into the sunshine and the more open country just north of Hite. Grandma's smile always came back with the sunshine and she began to breath normal again.

At Hite, we would most often cross the river on the ferryboat, but on occasion, and especially after the mill was shut down, we would cross in Grandpa's motorboat. Arth Chaffin charged $1.50 to take the pickup across, plus a small fee for each person. It was a very reasonable price, but for some of the locals like Grandpa, who had mining claims in the area and who crossed the river often, it was cheaper to keep a vehicle parked on each side of the river and run your own boat across.

Grandpa's boat was a small, wooden craft, highly lacquered with a tight little storage locker in the bow. It had capacity for four or five adults and a stray kid or two. It had a big aluminum-colored outboard engine clinging to the stern with hard, steel fingers. A couple of wooden oars were tucked under the seats – just in case.

Grandpa kept the boat tied with a chain in the willows a mile or more upriver from the Hite Ferry. It was at a wide place under the big ledge where there was room to park and leave his truck. He always told us kids he used a chain to tie the boat because he didn't want a damn beaver chewing through his rope. I suspect the real reason was that he could lock a chain and there was less chance of the boat being stolen or set adrift. And, a chain was less likely to chafe against the willows or rot in the hot, damp climate.

The beaver story played to my imagination, however, and Grandpa was eager to help. He would unlock the boat chain and then make a close inspection. He would wrinkle his brow dramatically as he held the chain up to the sunlight, and then he would say something like, "Yep, that damn beaver's been chewin' on the chain again. I'm sure glad I didn't use a rope."

I always looked hard to see if I could spot that trouble-making beaver. I always imagined him lurking nearby in the bushes with his shiny buckteeth all chipped up from chewing on that chain. I kept a sharp eye out, but I never did get to see him, and I was very disappointed.

Oh, how Grandma hated to cross the river in that little boat. As we got ready to cross over, she would stand and look out across that wide, muddy river, and she would just wilt. Grandpa would start the boat engine and let it idle to warm up, and then he would put Grandma and us kids into the boat and push us out into the edge of the water while he finished loading. There were always boxes of groceries, cans of gas, drill steels, truck parts, spare tires and whatever else he was taking across. He would wrap the beaver chain around his wrist to help hold us against the shore while he worked, and Grandma would start to panic. "Lorin … you be careful Lorin. Lorin … damn it, you be careful Lorin!"

Her river chant was one of the few times I ever heard her say "damn." Usually she said, "Oh, fiddle sticks," or "darn." Her use of the word underscored her level of panic and fear. She must have been truly terrified. Her handsome leading man, Rhett Butler Grandpa, was good at cussing and he always said cool stuff like, "Frankly my dear, I don't give a damn."

White Canyon

I expected cuss words from him, but to hear her say one was a rare thing indeed.

I remember watching with amazement as the little boat settled deeper and deeper into the water as it was loaded with people and supplies, the musty-smelling water coming closer and closer up the sides of the frail little craft. The boat had life preservers that were square seat cushions with naugahide handles. We all used one to sit on. I guessed that if the boat tipped over we were supposed to grab a seat cushion and hang on, but I don't remember anyone ever saying for sure.

With the boat finally loaded, Grandpa would clamber aboard. The boat would rock and Grandma would suck in her breath and dig her fingers into our clothes and soft skin. Grandpa would fumble with the steering arm and the throttle for a few seconds and the boat would begin to drift backwards down the river. Then, the engine would spit and sputter as she caught her breath and the boat would start to push against the current. As she caught her stride, the engine would growl deep in her throat, then hum like a vacuum cleaner. Grandpa would turn the boat with the prow pointed upstream, quartering into the waves, and layback on the throttle. The spinning prop would suck the back of the boat low into the water and the bow would rise up as she gained speed. I could feel the vibration of the engine through the wooden ribs of the Viking ship, and flecks of cool river spray touched my face and hands.

As we moved out into the full river current, an electric tingle would surge through my whole body and my legs would feel weak from shock and fear. Like Grandma, I hadn't learned to swim yet, and that vulnerability hung around my neck like a millstone. The dark water mocked my fear and made deepwater drowning sounds along the sides of the boat that slurped, smacked, gulped and gurgled. The river was toying with me. She was laughing at my fear of her and reminding me that I couldn't breathe under water. I was afraid, and I would grip the boat seat tightly and look out at waves that were almost shoulder high to little boys over the side of the boat. It was like looking over the side of a bathtub with the water on the outside.

Grandpa had to keep the bow turned upstream and into the current to keep the little boat from swamping. There was always the danger of floating logs and other debris in the channel and Grandpa would sit with a hand on the steering arm with his neck stretched high, chin in the air, watching the dark water come at us.

The river always looked a lot wider when we were sitting down in the boat and Grandma would close her eyes and hold on to our collars or the back of our belts with white knuckles. She would be whispering quietly under her breath, and I knew she was praying.

The little boat rose and fell and sometimes bucked in the water as it pushed through the river waves. Sometimes the rocking motion took my breath away, or tickled my little boy's belly like a roller coaster. From each side of the prow a long wake shaved off and flowed past to be swallowed by the current behind us. The sound of the humming engine echoed over the flat water and a thin blanket of blue smoke followed the boat across the river, the blue smoke blanket spreading low over the flat, dark water.

When we finally reached the far shore, Grandpa would beach the little craft into the mud as best he could and then jump out with the beaver chain in his hand. Sometimes he would make a big splash in the water and the little boat would tip dangerously. Grandma would gasp and then hurry to hand him a little boy and she would begin her river chant again. "Lorin … you be careful Lorin. Lorin … damn it Lorin … you be careful!"

And then we were on the sandy beach and safe again. Grandma would sigh gratefully and breathe deeply like she had been holding her breath for a long time. Grandpa would fuss with the boat and the supplies and Grandma would shoo us kids back through the willows and away from the muddy water. She would herd us out onto the dry warm sand of the desert where things were calm, safe and friendly. We were finally across the river and against those warm, red hills. We were at Grandma's house, and we were home.

White Canyon

12
The Long Way Around

In the early summer of 1952, just a few months after my family moved to White Canyon, Uncle Var went to Price to get supplies for the boardinghouse. Aunt Melba Winn and her two young daughters, Janis and Lauren, had been visiting with relatives in Carbon County and they caught a ride back to White Canyon with him. Janis was two and Lauren only three or four months old. It was crowded in the cab of the little pickup truck with two adults, two babies, diaper bags, pillows and blankets. The road was long and bumpy and the day was hot and sticky.

They reached Hite in the late afternoon and found the river running very high. The ferry cables were under water. The ferry operator told them he was sorry, but there was just no way he could take them across. The river was in full flood and it might be a few days before the ferry approaches could be repaired and the boat put back in service.

The news was a shock and a bitter disappointment. They were not prepared to spend the night and there were no tourist accommodations at Hite. So near and yet so far. Across the river they could see the uranium mill and the glint of trailer houses through the willows. The boardinghouse and the tent-roofed cabin that was Melba's home were just across the river in the trees. Husband and father, a warm shower, fresh milk, cookies, and a bed for the babies were just across the angry water. It would be dark soon.

Melba was in a tight spot, stranded with two little babies. She had three options. She could accept the hospitality of the ferry operator and his family and hope the water went down soon. Or, she could camp out in the cab of the pickup truck and endure until the crossing was safe, which might be a day or two or three. Or, she could saddle up and resume a back-breaking journey of another three hundred and thirty miles to go all the way around and approach White Canyon from the east.

To go around, they needed to go 110 miles on the dirt road back through Hanksville to the town of Green River. There, they could cross the Green River on the Green River bridge and drive east on Highway 6 to Crescent Junction. At Crescent Junction they would follow Highway 191 south to Moab and cross the Colorado River bridge there before continuing on to Monticello and Blanding. At Blanding they would take a dirt road to the west and it would be a good 75 miles over Elk Ridge and the Bears Ears to complete the circle. The journey around the horn would take all of eight hours, maybe nine or ten. The babies were already tired, dirty and fussy. Melba was worn out from the previous 170-mile and almost five hour journey over rough roads while balancing babies on her lap. Her supply of milk, cookies, clean diapers and good humor were running low. What to do?

As luck would have it, there was a gentleman nearby who kept a boat on the river. He worked for the federal government. His job was to monitor the river and keep tabs on the rate of flow, salinity, sedimentation, etc. He lived on the west side of the river near Hite. He had a nice little government-issue house that was painted white and sat on a rocky hill some distance above the ferry site. His wife and family lived there with him. The government water man was Elmer Carl Gerhart,

Mr. Gerhart was at the ferry site that fateful afternoon and saw Melba's predicament. Gallantly, he offered to take her across in his boat. He had a big government-issue motorboat with a very strong engine. He was on the river often and he knew his boat and the ways of the river.

It was risky business, and she knew it, but Melba was anxious to get back to her husband and the father of her little girls. She wanted to put her babies in their warm little beds on the other side of the river, and the thought of going all the way around was more than she could bear. So, she graciously accepted the man's offer. She said she wouldn't have done it, but he seemed so sure of himself, she decided it would be all right.

Uncle Var would have none of it. He tried vainly, and probably wisely, to talk them out of attempting the hazardous crossing. But Melba had made up her mind and she would not be swayed.

They had to hurry. It was late afternoon, almost dark, and the hazards of the crossing multiplied with the shadows. There were things floating in the flood that were not friendly to boats and boat passengers. The gathering darkness would make the obstacles more difficult to see.

They loaded some of the more perishable grocery items into the boat, then Melba and the babies took their seats. The boat's Captain came aboard with confidence, competence and courage. He pointed the prow into the boiling water and they struck out into the flood.

Melba held the baby tight, wrapped in a blanket. The government boatman steered the boat with one hand and held two-year-old Janis by the wrist with the other hand. Janis screamed all the way across the river. Not because she was afraid of the boat or the water, but because she didn't want to sit by the strange man who held her wrist while steering the boat.

Whole trees were floating down the river and the channel was filled with snags, driftwood, ocean waves, foam and floating debris. The boatman was skilled and he dodged the obstacles. The big engine dug deep in the muddy water and pushed like a torpedo. The boat rode high over the swelling crests and smashed through the waves with spray flying high. Melba hugged baby Lauren on her lap and tried to console her second screaming daughter. But she had to hold the boat seat with one hand as the craft bounced and skipped over the rolling waves. Var watched from the western shore and paced anxiously. He fully understood the danger, and it was probably harder to stand and watch than to participate in the drama.

People on the White Canyon side of the river were alerted that a daring beach landing was about to take place by the echo of the boat engine and the siren wail of the little girl who struggled to free herself from the iron grip of the boat's Captain. They ran out by the riverbank and watched as the landing craft plowed toward the shore.

Mr. Gerhart was a good pilot and he got them safely across. He took them upstream to the mouth of White Canyon Wash and drove the boat up the flooded creek channel and right to the back of the boardinghouse. That was something that normally couldn't be done because White Canyon wash usually ran only a trickle. The flood had become so bad that a caterpillar was being used to make a dike to protect the buildings from the rising water. My family never saw a worse flood in the years they were on the desert.

The boatman unloaded his precious cargo, then turned back into the flood and made it safely back across the river to his own wife and family. To my family, Elmer Gerhart was a Knight in shining armor, a man of courage and chivalry more gallant than Sir Walter Raleigh. A man who did more to help a lady than simply spread his cloak over a puddle.

Melba was thrilled to be home, but not prepared for the reception she received. Instead of being happy to see her and the babies, everyone kept chewing her out for being so brash and so bold as to attempt the river crossing.

Melba Winn is a strong woman. She's a good woman too and I've always admired her spunk and free spirit. She has a deep love for the red desert and it has never held any terrors for her. She would have made a great pioneer. When things got scary, when the chips were down and it was time to stand up and be counted, I know she would have spit in the devil's eye and drove the wagon down the Hole In The Rock trail.

When Uncle Var saw they had safely stormed the beach on the far shore, he drove the three hundred and thirty miles to go around the flood. It was a long and lonely trek that took him all night. He reached the boardinghouse early the next morning from the east. The water was still high and the ferry still closed. He had spent the whole night, and hundreds of miles of weary travel, to gain the distance of about four hundred yards.

Notes:

Thank you to Chuck Gerhart, who called the author on the phone and gave him the name of his father, the government boatman who challenged the river.

13
North Wash

There was a special place on my red desert when I was a kid. It was a place where all the angels of the desert gathered: towering ledges, tapestry walls, monolithic sandstone sculptures, clean red sand, cotton ball clouds and clear blue sky. It was a magnificent canyon of rare beauty that wore a humble and unassuming name. It was probably Cass Hite who first started calling the place North Wash. To me, North Wash was always the highlight of our desert travels.

In my humble opinion, Zion's Park, Canyonlands, Monument Valley, Arches, and the Grand Staircase Escalante, have nothing on the place. The canyon is a wonderland of marvelous rock formations. The texture, colors, and the feel of the place is awe-inspiring.

Today North Wash is still one of the treasures of the red desert, but most people don't know it because it isn't marked as a scenic wonder on their maps. Thousands of people zip through the canyon every year at 60 miles an hour and don't even see it.

John Wesley Powell didn't see it the first time he sailed past. Or, if he did, he didn't mention it. The canyon was narrow and twisted where it met the Colorado and rock walls near the river shielded the canyon from view. North Wash flows not a trickle in dry weather, and it went unnoticed or unmentioned by Major Powell and his river boatmen who camped near its mouth in July 1869. It was however, the best pack trail and wagon route to the river for many miles. And, the canyon had been an Indian highway for millennia.

On his second exploration of Glen Canyon in 1872, Major Powell's party camped again near the mouth of North Wash and did repair work on some of the boats. Major Powell considered the mouth of the Dirty Devil to be the upper boundary of Glen Canyon and the flat place in the sand at the mouth of North Wash was the first good campsite in the canyon. There is a famous Jack Hillers photograph of the exploring party working on an overturned boat at the base of a towering butte that is now across the lake from the Hite Marina. The butte is below the Wrinkle Rocks at the mouth of North Wash and now stands out of the lake like an island. It is at the very end of the long sandstone ridge that is the platform for the Hite overlook on Highway 95.

White Canyon

In the 1880s North Wash was called Crescent Creek. It wouldn't be North Wash until the early twentieth century. The origin of the name, North Wash, can be understood when one knows the history of the place and looks at a map of the area.

Jack Hillers 1872 photo of John Wesley Powell's men
repairing boats at the mouth of North Wash

From Cass Hite's old cabin, there were two possible trails out of the river canyon to the west. One was Trachyte wash, the other Crescent Creek. Of the two, Crescent Creek was the better trail. It was relatively flat bottomed, there were good, cold-water springs along the route, and the trail climbed out of the canyon a few miles closer to Hanksville and the town of Green River.

Crescent Creek wasn't a creek at all, but more properly a dry wash. It was the wash north of Trachyte and north of Hite City, and therefore called "the north wash" by people who lived at Hite. I can clearly hear old Cass Hite telling his brothers, "I'm goin' ta Green River fer beer an' beans. I'll be takin' the trail up the north wash. Be back sometime next week."

North Wash

The desert around Hanksville is open and exposed to the sky. It is wide and empty and warmed by the sun. A person can see for miles in any direction and it is surely beautiful. The desert breeze chases tumbleweeds across the sand flats. Heat shimmers on distant horizons.

Nothing is hidden there. The desert can keep no secrets in the flat country. Clumps of tamarack and twisted cottonwood tell the whole world where the water is. Range cows and antelope beat dusty trails to the best forage spots and salt licks. Bumpy little roads betray mineral deposits, mines and hidden homesteads. And when an old cow goes down to stay, her sun-bleached bones can be seen for half-a-mile. Billowing white clouds, black desert ravens and nosy little airplanes look down on everything that happens.

In the canyons things are different, and that was the charm of North Wash to me. In the canyons the secrets of the desert are kept. The walls of the canyons are a library of history, geology, mineralogy, paleontology and archaeology. All preserved on pages of eternal stone. Bound, sealed and indexed by Mother Nature. North Wash, and other canyons like her, are treasure boxes.

As a kid, I was charmed by North Wash. She is timeless, mysterious and ever changing. Around every bend the scenery changes and the ragged edge of the sky is different. Dozens of side canyons, rocky terraces, grottos, sand slides, potholes and shadows beg to be noticed and explored. Every terrace holds a promise. Every rim shields a mystery. Every cave hides a pirate's treasure.

As the road approaches North Wash from Hanksville, it drops down into the channel of the wash just before the walls of the canyon begin to rise from the sand. Another mile and the road begins to snuggle down into the warm bosom of Mother Earth. The long vistas are suddenly gone and the yellow sand turns to stone. The desert stands vertical and she comes in close.

The canyon walls are warm and they wrap you like a blanket. The warmth draws you to it in ways you don't understand. Even the colors are warm and inviting: varying shades of red, brown, orange, pink and black. The walls radiate heat borrowed from the sun and energy from the eternal furnace at the core of the Earth.

Unlike the open desert country, the canyons hold you close. The desert enfolds you. The horizon is in the clouds at the top of the ledges and the tapestry walls take your eyes upward like the long, stained-glass windows of a cathedral. Deep in the canyon everything is different: the light, the stillness, the vegetation, the echo of the wind – the very feel of the desert.

White Canyon

The closeness is comforting. Canyon walls are the strong sheltering arms of the wilderness.

It is a wonderland. Varied and wondrous gems of rare vegetation cling to rock walls or burst forth through cracks in the stone. Cactus and bunchgrass stake claims to sandy pockets. Solitary desert flowers stretch long stems skyward and dot the sandy places with scarlet, royal blue and Sego Lilly white. Ancient Juniper trees dig gnarled toes into crevices in the rocks and hang on for another season. Pools of rainwater reflect a blue sky from potholes in the rocks, while the shadows of clouds sneak silently over the ledges and move across the canyon like ghostly phantoms.

Deep in the ledges, masonry walls peek out from the shadows and hide under overhanging rims. Ancient chips of pottery spill down and burrow deep in the red sand. The ghosts of the Anasazi leave no tracks in the soft sand to betray the sacred places. High sandstone walls shelter the ruins from prying eyes and winter storms.

There are other ghosts in the canyons, deer tracks from deer never seen, and the spirits of extinct species. There are bones of dinosaurs, broken and scattered, and graven images of long-dead mountain sheep carved on the rocks and lacquered with desert varnish. Petrified trees speak of cool shady forests. Tiny marine fossils suggest ocean floors and sandy beaches.

An angel's feather is sometimes found there, lightly touched down and waiting for a desert breeze to take it back to heaven. Some angel feathers are blue. Some are soft brown or gray, fading to white around the edges. Some are ebony black. Some angel feathers are flaming orange in color, like the under-wing of a Flicker.

Sparrow Hawks, ravens and eagles nest in the ledges and soar through the canyons on thermal rivers of warm air. Great owls sleep, deep in shady crags, and wait for the night to return. Swallows build little cliff houses of tiny mud bricks and scurry through the air on impatient errands. Gaggles of Pinion Jays scoot from tree to tree, arguing and giggling, all talking at once. They are the gossipy feathered sentinels of the canyons, scattering to the ledges to sound an alarm whenever an outsider comes near.

North Wash is alive, and she's been alive since God first traced her outline with his finger in the mud of creation. I love to go there, and when I do, my heart soars with the eagles.

In the 1950s, a special treat was traveling through the canyon in the dark. North Wash is majesty in the daylight, and magic in the dark of night. As my Grandpa's little truck dropped down into the head of North Wash in the night, I would sit on the edge of my seat and stare in awe at the gemstone-sprinkled sky and the dark shadows of the approaching canyon walls. I would tremble with excitement as the desert began to rise up around us, dark and silent. The road slowly twisted into the shallow depths of the upper canyon and the sand flats were left behind. We were descending into a great crack in the earth where everything was dark, empty and quiet.

And yet, there was nothing ominous or scary about the descent. North Wash was my friend. I was drawn to her and she held no terrors for me. She sometimes looked dark and foreboding in the night, and her emptiness echoed from the canyon walls, but the feel of her was not like that. In spite of her sometimes-gloomy countenance, I could see past her wrinkled brow, and I knew her heart was soft.

In North Wash, the old road crossed and re-crossed the wash three dozen times in a span of only sixteen miles. There were no culverts or bridges. The road twisted and turned, dodging boulders and cottonwood trees. Sometimes it passed very close to the towering rock walls of the canyon. Sometimes if followed the gravely bottom of the wash for several hundred yards.

I remember the harsh, irreverent splash of water in the stillness of the night as we crossed and re-crossed that desert wash. I remember the sudden flash of light and color on the dark walls of the canyon as the headlights reflected from the puddles. I remember the strong and steady thump of that little engine as we traveled through that nighttime desert wonderland. The canyon was dark and deathly quiet. The sounds of our passing echoed far into the night. The only sound in all the world was the heartbeat of that little Chevrolet and the rowdy splash of water as she dragged her feet through the puddles. It was an irreverent intrusion and the tranquility of that lonesome place was violated. Sometimes I felt almost guilty.

And then, from deep in the shadows, I could feel the Anasazi watching as we passed by. Those spirits of the desert had lived in the canyon many years ago, in a world far removed from pickup trucks with glowing headlights. I wondered what they might think of us as we passed by them in the dark.

I remember the moon smiling down, peeking at us through the clouds and casting long, silver shadows on the ledges. There was one brilliant, summer night in particular when great billowing clouds, shining in the moonlight, sneaked silently across the night sky to capture a huge, full moon as it passed slowly overhead. The clouds toyed with the moon, cat and mouse, catching and releasing, then catching the moon again. The shadows on the canyon walls dimmed and then burst forth many shades brighter as the cosmic kidnappings played out. It was a wondrous thing to see, a spectacle I will never forget. Those great, billowing clouds glowed in the moonlight like they were lit from within – bright, milky nightlights in the desert sky. The canyon was almost as bright as day and we could easily have traveled the full length without using the headlights. I've never seen anything like it.

Sometimes we camped out in the canyon overnight. Grandpa liked to camp out and he always had his camping gear in the back of the truck when he left town. North Wash was one of his favorite camping places and Hog Spring was his favorite spot. It was a pretty place when it belonged to us. We camped there often.

The campsite was tucked into the sheltering ledges at the mouth of Hog Spring Canyon. There was a thin grove of cottonwood trees, a smattering of green grass, and soft, red dirt to camp on. The spring came from a pipe driven into the sandy creek bank from which splashed a weak but steady flow of cold, sweet water.

The old spring isn't there anymore. Road construction and attempts to "enhance the flow" killed it in the 1970s. Today, Grandpa's old campsite is covered by a paved parking area, a visitor kiosk, a wooden footbridge, picnic tables and civilized restrooms. But that's okay, Grandpa would understand. The highway department worked hard to preserve what they could of the natural balance and the wildness of the place, and they did a good job. It's still a pretty place to visit. It is a good rest stop and a safe, domesticated place for a picnic lunch. There are benches, tables, awnings, and trashcans.

I remember one of our camping trips to Hog Spring especially. I was nine or ten years old, a growing boy, and I was starving when we finally stopped to make camp. It was late afternoon and I hadn't eaten anything since early that morning. It was a rare thing for us to have candy, snacks or soda pop when we traveled with Grandpa. He was from the old school and the food was in the back of the truck in a grub box. There was plenty to eat, but it was no-nonsense stuff: canned goods, homemade bread, potatoes, eggs and onions. Nobody ate anything until camp was made and the grill was hot.

That particular afternoon, Grandpa made a smoky fire of brush and dead cottonwood limbs and cooked our supper in a big skillet over the fire. It was a Thanksgiving feast of bacon, fried ham, pork and beans and creamed corn all mixed together into a bubbling stew. No meal I ever ate tasted better. Grandpa was a good cook over a campfire, and practiced. I remember soaking up that manna in the wilderness with thick slices of Grandma's homemade bread and butter, and I rejoiced. I might not starve to death after all. My little belly purred as Grandpa's prospector stew put the fire out.

North Wash

Grandpa often mixed things together when he cooked over a fire. He seemed to take pride in cooking a whole meal in a single skillet all at once. It was like a contest to see how resourceful he could be. He told us that when he was prospecting out on the desert, he once fried eggs and potatoes on the blade of a shovel when he forgot his skillet. Sometimes he boiled eggs in the coffeepot to save water.

After dinner and before it got dark, brother Reed and I ventured into that great rock shelter near Hog Spring that serves as a gallery for the Moki Queen. We often stopped to pay our respects and it was always a walk on sacred ground to me. The Moki Queen is a magnificent rock art panel, a red ochre bridge to a distant past. She is an impressive pictograph, one of the best anywhere.

The Moki Queen is dressed in royal robes, and she stands stately and regal in her appointed place among the rocks. She is the very heart and soul of the canyon and the embodiment of the human experience on the whole of the desert. The ancient artist was a master. In that wild and natural setting, with only sandstone and raw mineral pigment for medium, Rembrandt or Michelangelo could not have captured the essence of the human spirit with more power.

The pictograph is life-sized and is done in a unique style found only in the eastern Utah area. Scholars call paintings of this type Barrier Canyon Style, and they are thought to be thousands of years old. Only a few dozen examples are known to exist and the Moki Queen is one of the best. She is painted in red, and appears to be a person wearing a long robe with a crown of white dots outlining her head. That she might be female is purely speculative, but since the early pioneers had crowned her a queen, we always dealt with her on that basis.

A double row of white dots drape over the Queen's upper body from her shoulders, adorning her neck like an Egyptian royal necklace, while solid white lines cascade down the front of her robe. In typical Barrier Canyon style, the figure has no arms or legs. She may have represented a spirit or a deity. To her left, a dog, also done in red paint, stands by her. Over the years, the legs and ears of the dog have grown very faint. It appears that the appendages of the dog were painted with a different batch of paint that was a thinner mix, or even a substitute pigment. Because the legs of the dog are not readily apparent, we boys always imagined the dog to be a huge coiled snake about to strike that helpless Indian princess. We even imagined that the beautiful, snake-bitten Indian woman was buried somewhere close at the feet of the pictograph, her painted likeness serving as her grave marker.

White Canyon

In spite of our youthful imagining that the pictograph might be a grave marker, we never tried to dig to find out. None of my family would ever condone grave robbing. My brothers and I were taught at an early age to respect and protect all ruins and remains, ancient, and more recent.

There is a hole in the Moki Queen's chest and another near her feet that might be old bullet wounds. The bullet didn't hurt her, and she wears that scar of disrespect nobly. The blemish preserves forever the shame and the heartless stupidity of that soulless creature that could have done such a thing. It appears that the bullets hit the wall a long time ago, probably back during the gold rush days of the 1890s when nothing on the desert was sacred.

We stopped to visit the Moki Queen often when I was a kid, and I always approached her in reverent wonder. It was like visiting a shrine or a mausoleum. A great sandstone cave envelops the painting and it is a vital and powerful part of the ancient monument. When you step inside that great cathedral of stone, deep inside the canyon wall, everything is suddenly quiet. A veil of seclusion is drawn. A huge sand dune in the mouth of the cave helps preserve the reverence and shields those paying homage from the outside world. It is shady, cool and calm inside the cave. The air is still and voices echo.

The Moki Queen - Author photo

North Wash

As a person approaches the painting, her presence surrounds you. She reaches out and takes you back five thousand years. You are suddenly in her world and under her spell. She holds you there in quiet veneration. To stand before her is communion with an ancient past. She is a solid, tangible link to a whole race of vanished people. The power of the humanity she represents, the spirit and soul of those ancient desert dwellers, radiates from her. For a time she holds you in a wrap of reverence and mystery. Then you walk away, and step out into the sunlight and the twenty-first century again.

The Moki Queen still looks out at the world from her vantage point deep in the vastness of her rocky sanctuary. Most tourists zip on past, towing boats or trailers as they head for Lake Powell. Most never see her there, standing back in the shadows, watching, as they fly past.

We camped out that night right there in the dirt. We spread our bedding out on the ground on a large tarp that Grandpa used to cover the camping gear in the back of the truck. It was quiet there that night. We had the canyon all to ourselves. No cars came down that winding dirt road and there were no other people anywhere.

It was a beautiful bright night. The sky was dusted with millions of twinkling stars. Everything was quiet. Even the sky was quiet. There was no far-off rumble of jet engines or the faint shriek of metal wings in the night. There were no smoky contrails, those unsightly airplane tracks, to disfigure the night sky and hide the planets. The only contrail in the heavens was that wide, shining band of the Milky Way, that magnificent ribbon of diamond dust stretching far into eternity. It was a night sky the Anaszai would have recognized.

A person must spend a night out on the sand to understand just how splendid a desert night like that can be. On such a night, stillness settles like a mist that covers everything. You can actually feel the quiet. Out in the darkness everything is hushed as if the desert is holding its breath. People speak in soft, whispered tones without realizing they are doing it. Silence fills the canyon, then evaporates up into the night, not to be disturbed. The stars, moon and clouds hang quietly, reverently overhead, stillness echoing from the canyon walls.

If you listen closely … you will swear you can faintly hear moon shadows dragging over the slickrock, and horned toads breathing through their little noses out on the sand dunes.

White Canyon

14
Grandma's House

In July 1954, after the uranium mill shut down and White Canyon Town was gone, Lorin and Bertha became homesteaders. Uranium homesteaders. The place they picked for their homestead was an isolated spot near the north end of the dirt airfield. It was a mile or more north of where the town had been, two or three miles south of where the Hite Marina is today. Their pioneer home was nestled in the mouth of a small, narrow and unnamed little canyon, a sheltered cove tucked back in the warm red hills. There were no trees there and it was not an especially beautiful place, but Grandpa had discovered a small spring in the rocks that would provide clean fresh water, a commodity as precious as uranium on the desert.

They were not squatters in the truest sense of the word. They had somehow acquired official permission or a government permit to set up housekeeping on the public lands. It's not surprising. Government agents were quite accommodating to anyone seriously searching for uranium. Lorin and Bertha never held a deed to the ground, but Uncle Sam was their absentee landlord. It was a great arrangement. Rent was free and they treated the place like they owned it.

They didn't build a real house. In keeping with the transient, make-do-until-you-strike-it-rich philosophy of the uranium boom, they put together two twelve by twenty-four-foot little wooden buildings. In fact, one of the little buildings had been Uncle Nate and Aunt Lorraine's house. They simply put the little shed-house on skids, wrapped a chain around it and dragged it to the new homestead site with a caterpillar.

The shed-houses were exactly like most of the other little dwellings that had prevailed in White Canyon. The cabins were without insulation of any kind and with no electrical wiring. The floors were covered with cheap linoleum and the roofs were rolled asphalt. The walls were made of one-inch boards. Plywood was still something new and not readily available back then. Tarpaper lined the exterior walls to seal the cracks and gaps. There was no sheet rock or plaster on the inside. Raw wood was exposed and slivery. No paint was wasted on the inside or the outside. Everything was done as cheaply as possible.

The two buildings were pushed close together but there was no door to connect them. One was used for sleeping and the other as a kitchen and living quarters. To go to bed at night, they took the coal oil lamp from the kitchen table and carried it outside and into the other building where the beds were.

It was a temporary campsite and they made little attempt to make it a permanent home. Everything was field expedient like the military-inspired company camp where the uranium mill had been. They expected to be there for only a short time and they put little effort into decorating the place or installing good furniture.

They made do with old and pioneer-worthy articles that could be discarded at the end of the adventure without being hauled the many miles back to civilization. Their good furniture and most household goods were left in their home in Wellington or put in storage.

The shed-houses sat on improvised foundations made of wooden beams, cinderblocks, flat rocks and wooden wedges that held the structures slightly elevated above the dirt. Rock slabs and boards served as steps. The screen doors were store-bought. The kitchen sported a small propane cook stove and a small wood-burning stove to provide heat in the wintertime. The other prominent article of furniture was a rickety old table that hid its head under a red and white checkered oilcloth table covering. A coal oil lamp sat proudly in the middle of the table. Cheap, metal-framed and cotton-stuffed kitchen chairs surrounded the table. The corners of the chairs were worn through and little boys delighted in digging the cotton stuffing out through little holes in the coverings.

The cupboards were portable, closet-type affairs. Ancient china closets without glass, might best describe them. These were assisted in their domestic duties by a few wooden boxes, shelves made of rough planking, and assorted nails and wire hooks that held cooking spoons, tubs, pans, pokers and fly swatters.

There was no grass, asphalt or cement for miles, and when the wind blew there was no barrier in the world that could hold back the red dust. The red dust stained everything. The off-white linoleum of the floor was stained red where everyone walked. The foot traffic ground the red stain into the linoleum and it could not be scrubbed out. The linoleum against the walls and under the furniture was still white, and the contrast always made the floor look dirty. Grandma was meticulous and she scrubbed the floor often, but the red stain defied her best efforts. Curtains, towels and underclothes also took on the red cast. The redness invaded the fabric with such tenacity that it could not be washed out. Outside the house, even truck tires, fence posts, sage brush leaves and weeds, blushed red with the all-pervading stain.

Grandma's House

Grandpa tapped the little spring in the canyon and with pioneer ingenuity and a lot of pipe and guy wires, he brought the little trickle of water right to the house. He then rigged up an ingenious hot water shower facility. He ran water from the little spring into a series of clean, fifty-five gallon drums that he suspended overhead on stout, heavy planking. During the day the hot desert sun warmed the water almost to the point of being too hot for us kids. Every afternoon we enjoyed a nice, warm shower in the special outdoors bathhouse Grandpa had rigged up. Of course the place did offered some privacy. The open-air shower had board walls and even a wooden-pallet floor to keep people up and out of the red dirt. It was an ingenious creation and much appreciated. The barrels would slowly refill overnight and heat in the sun again the next day. By late afternoon the water was hot and the shower was ready.

Grandma's House - 1955. Lorin and Bertha standing between the buildings.
Courtesy of Maurine Dorman

White Canyon

It got terribly hot in White Canyon during the summer months. People without air conditioning would simply wilt and swelter. We all shaded up in the middle of the day. The river canyon held heat like an oven. The hot air drew steam from the river and the steamy air was as thick as soup and tasted like tamarack bushes. The red sand got so hot it would burn your feet right through your shoes. With no electricity to run a fan, the house would get unbearably hot. In the middle of the day we often sat outside in the shade of the house where Grandma would read to us or tell us stories.

Grandpa would tell us stories too, but unlike Grandma, he always tried to pass his stories off as the gospel truth. It took me a few years to catch on that he wasn't always telling me the real deal. He did tell some funny stories that I've retold for many years.

For instance: he once said that he was prospecting over by Fry Canyon one afternoon, and it got so hot that the buzzards were leaving smoke trails in the sky like those new-fangled jet airplanes. He said the sun was so hot he could smell the heat-singed feathers burning from half-a-mile away. He also said he left the engine of his jeep running while he collected some rock samples, and when he came back to the jeep, a big lizard had crawled up inside the exhaust pipe and was lying there enjoying the shade.

A favorite story of his was that the lizards in White Canyon all carried a lump of horse manure in their teeth. He said they would run a little ways over the scorching sand, then throw the horse biscuit down and hurry and stand on it to keep the hot sand from burning their little feet. Now that was something I wanted to see.

I collected an armload of mummified horse do-do and offered a chunk to every lizard I met. The pious, self-respecting lizards all looked at me like I was crazy and refused to touch the stuff. Not to be deterred, I scattered some little equine shredded wheat biscuits near the lizards and stepped back and watched and waited. No luck. I decided that maybe the scented snippets of deteriorating donkey dung were too large for the stupid lizards, so I tiptoed back and crumbed them up. Still no luck. The snooty lizards wouldn't do the trick for me. Finally, in complete disgust, I decided that the smart-aleky lizards around Grandma's house were insolent, no-account good-for-nothings and I chased them out of the dooryard throwing rocks.

When I told Grandpa about it, he laughed and said he wasn't surprised. He said Lizards are embarrassed to carry horse biscuits in their shiny little teeth if they know people are watching. He told me I would have to hide and sneak up on them to see them do the trick.

Grandma's House

I spent the next couple of days peeking around corners at unsuspecting lizards while I baited them with tempting morsels. I selected only the finest of specimens, those nice firm lumps of fossilized pony poop that I was sure a fat lizard wouldn't be able to resist. I walked around for the better part of a week with my pockets full of odious and crumbling horse biscuit crumbs. But alas, I never did get to see a fat lizard run with a horse turd in his teeth. Grandpa said he had seen it lots of times, so I knew it was true. Grandpa said maybe it just wasn't hot enough the week I was there.

There was a lot of old horse manure scattered around that little desert cove where Grandpa put his house, and no one seemed to know where it came from. I never did see a horse out there on the desert. In retrospect, the horse biscuits may have been semi-fossilized coprolites, old-time dung-relics from the cowboy and Indian days, preserved by the dry desert environment.

Grandpa was always teasing us kids, and the horse biscuit lizard story is just one example. He tormented the little girls by showing them his broken and crooked index finger and telling them stories about how pretty it was. He always had something going and it was a rare thing for one of the kids to get one over on him. But it happened once in a while.

One day, Uncle Jack's little daughter Lauren, who was three or four years old at the time, came into Grandma's house, walked up to Grandpa with a disgusted look on her baby face, put her hands on her hips, stuck her little chin out, batted her long eyelashes, and said, "You got hose poop under you house." She then took him by the finger and made him go outside and get down on his knees and look. Sure enough … there under the cabin was a dried-up, mummified old horse turd. Lauren stood by in utter disgust and saintly indignation while he dug it out from beneath the house and properly disposed of it. Grandpa laughed about that for years. He had been teasing her that morning and she had gotten back at him, big time. Nothing could be more demeaning than to have "Hose poop under you house."

There was no place in the world where the nights were brighter than in White Canyon. And it was during those glorious desert nights that we boys got to know our grandparents best. One of the advantages of not having electricity and television was that people talked to each other. Like the Anasazi, our grandparents would sit outside under the stars and tell us stories at night. It was a wonderful and precious opportunity to get to know them.

We would sit outside in the cool air and the soft, silver glow of the moon and talk quietly. We would marvel at the sparkling gemstone stars and watch the moon shadows play over that great sandstone wall across the river. Crickets would serenade us from deep in the shadows and frogs would bark from down by the river.

Grandpa would sit in the moonlight on his hammock and point out all the different constellations to us kids. He would tell us all about them and have us stand behind him while he traced their outline in the sky with his finger. I tried hard, but I just couldn't make out most of them. I've always had a world-class imagination, but Scorpio and Pisces were beyond my abilities. I could see Orion's belt, but I could never figure out where Orion was. The same went for Leo the lion. Grandpa assured me he was there, but like the boat-chain-chewing beaver down by the river, I never got to see him, try as I might. I did learn about the big and little dippers, I could see them all right, and I learned how to locate the North Star.

Grandpa would give us the Native American star-vision test. There are three stars that make up the handle of the Big Dipper. Very near the middle star there is a very faint little spot of light that can be seen only if you have good eyes and look very carefully. He said when he was a boy on the Ute reservation, the Utes always said that if a boy could see that dim little star he would be a good hunter. I could see it and I was proud. I couldn't wait to be a good hunter. But sadly, our Native American friends sometimes speak with forked tongues. I loved to hunt, but I was never any good at it. Being able to see that little star didn't seem to help me out at all.

Grandpa said his uranium company was named after a constellation, The Southern Cross, but we were too far north to see it. He said it could be seen in Mexico and South America. He said it looked like the cross over a church house. I always hoped I could see it someday, but I never have.

The days were long and it was a lot of fun staying at grandma's house in the mouth of that little canyon. We boys chased lizards, made castles in the sand, climbed around in the rocks, rolled old tires down sandy slopes, and pounded hundreds of rusty nails into old boards.

There was a tremendous pile of old scrap lumber from the torn-down uranium mill that littered the mouth of the canyon. Grandpa had salvaged all of the radioactive remnants of good lumber he could, to use as material for his mining and pioneering projects. There were also coffee cans full of rusty, also-salvaged nails. Reed and I spend hours pounding the bent nails back into the salvaged lumber where the nails had come from in the first place. No one seemed to mind. I guess the project kept us occupied and Grandma could keep track of us by the constant rap, rap, rap of the hammers.

Grandma's House

Sometimes Grandma would take us for walks. She would take us on little nature hikes where she would point out all the little plants and flowers and tell us all about them. Sometimes we would look for pretty rocks. She liked to look for pretty rocks and White Canyon was full of them. There were places near her house where little buttons of multi-colored chert and quartzite were sprinkled out over the ground like spilled jellybeans. The rock candies sparkled in the hot sun and they were warm to the touch. Little boys had to stop and pee often when they filled their pockets with hot rocks.

Large chunks of petrified wood, sometimes whole tree trunks, lay scattered and broken in the red sand with the ancient bark turned to stone. The interiors of some of the tree fragments were magnificent, all the colors of the rainbow, and some had well-defined tree rings still clearly visible.

There were many small fragments of highly sculptured sandstone, weather-beaten little anomalies with dimples like rain drop impressions, or worm holes or odd bumps and ridges. With a little imagination, some looked like small animals or little people sculpted by the wind and water. They were always fun to find and Grandma kept a couple of the little animal sculptures on a knick-knack shelf in her home in Wellington for many years. I keep them now, as souvenirs and reminders of her, and her desert home.

Sometimes Indian relics were found in the area. It was not unusual to discover an arrowhead now and then. Some of the men who went into the canyons prospecting for uranium found complete pottery vessels and brought them back to town for show and tell. The man who ran the ferryboat had a lizard made of Anasazi pottery he said he found somewhere up in White Canyon. He showed it to us when we crossed on the ferryboat. It was painted black and white like the pottery fragments littering the ground around the old Moki fort.

There wasn't a lot of Indian stuff right near Grandma's house, but I tried hard to find an arrowhead just the same. One day I was up in the rocks above her house looking for an arrowhead when I found a rectangular piece of webbing. It was sticking out of the sand in a shady alcove against a ledge. To me it looked like a fragment of a thick cargo strap or a piece of belting from Grandpa's uranium machinery that lay scattered in the yard far below. I couldn't imagine how it got all the way up there. It was tightly woven and had little stripes of faded red and orange braided through it. The red dirt stuck to it tenaciously and it looked like it had been in the ground for a long time. I tossed it aside and continued my search for an arrowhead.

Many years later, while viewing archaeological collections buried deep in a basement at the University of Utah, it dawned on me that what

White Canyon

I had found that day was a Basketmaker sandal. It was probably in the neighborhood of two thousand years old and perfectly preserved. I was eight or nine years old when the Ancient Ones presented that gift to me, and I hadn't recognized what it was. I had innocently cast it aside and left it to the mercy of the lake. Oh, to turn back the years!

Jack and Melba moved a camp trailer into the same little cove where Grandma's house was, and they too lived there for a time. Jack was still in charge of operations for the Smith Mining Company and his people were still drilling and exploring. Janis, their oldest daughter, tells of sitting on a hill above Grandma's house when she was five or six years old, alone with her thoughts and feelings.

She was a beautiful and imaginative little girl, with love in her heart and stars in her eyes. That magnificent river canyon lay before her, open and inviting like the red rock Garden of Eden that it was. She looked down at all the sparkling little jellybean stones shining in the sun and pretended they were jewels. In her child's mind, she was the Queen of the Canyon, sitting on a sandstone throne and looking out over her jewels and her realm.

Janis is a true child of the desert and she was different from all the rest of us. At the age of six, White canyon was the only home she knew or could remember. She had been nurtured and reared in that red rock garden. No one could ever submit a better claim to ownership of that river canyon than she.

White Canyon really was her kingdom. The sculpted rock garden was her magnificent throne room. The sandstone ledges the walls of her castle. The mighty Colorado her castle moat. Sunbeams and angels were her attendants. The desert breeze stood by to do her bidding. The sun bowed low to kiss her crown, her beautiful golden hair, and she didn't need to pretend. She really was The Queen of White Canyon.

Jack and Melba Winn moved the family to Texas in 1956. They were in exile for many long years, but finally came home to settle in Moab. Texas was a good place to make a living, but the red desert was always home. Cousin Janis Winn York lives with her family in Moab too, and she's still The Queen of White Canyon, as far as I'm concerned.

Janis and Grandma developed a special relationship over the years. When Janis was in Texas they sent kisses through the mail and held hands over the long-distance telephone. Though often far apart, they bonded in a way that was wonderful to see. When they were together, that older woman and that pretty young daughter communicated heart-to-heart with simple smiles and nods. They were girls who shared birthday cards, recipes, books, letters, and DNA. They also shared a common heart. They understood each other. Their eyes said it all. They didn't have to speak.

The most exciting thing about Grandma's house for little boys was the airfield. The house was very near the end of the dirt runway that launched and recovered the fragile little airplanes that frequented the area. The town was gone by then, but there were still a lot of miners, prospectors and government functionaries flying in and out of the canyon.

We could hear the echo of the airplane engines rippling from the canyon walls a long time before we could see the planes. We were at the very end of the airfield and the aircraft would be just above the ground when they flashed past us whether they were landing or taking off.

Whenever we heard an airplane Reed and I would run to the house and get Grandma by the hand and make her run out to the edge of the airfield with us. Grandma wasn't as excited about the whole thing as we were, but she had threatened to put us out of our misery if we ever went out there by ourselves, so she was a good sport about going with us.

White Canyon airfield in front of Grandma's house
facing south toward the abandoned White Canyon town site
Author photo - December, 1959

White Canyon

It was more fun than Disneyland to see one of those little planes barreling down that runway toward us. The engine would be screaming, the propeller flashing in the sun and a great billowing cloud of dust would chase the little craft toward us. We would jump up and down and hold our tickled little bellies as the plane raced to outrun the dust cloud.

The roar of the engine would get louder and louder and the plane would get bigger and bigger and then leap into the air just before it got to us. We would wave excitedly as the plane roared at us, and then we would duck as the noise and the prop wash slammed past. Sometimes, people in the plane would wave back as they shot past, which completely made our day and tickled our little bellies even more.

As the little plane escaped skyward, the dust cloud would give up the chase and swirl across the end of the runway near where we were standing. The thick cloud would skid to a stop against the bushes at the edge of the airfield and a fine red power would sprinkle down on everything. We would sometimes choke and cough and Grandma would hold her apron up over her mouth and nose. Then we would all laugh.

The sound of the engine would be deafening as the metal eagle screamed past. And then, as it clawed for altitude to clear the ledges, a booming echo would chase the plane up the river. The echo would bounce back and forth across the canyon as the plane gained distance and altitude.

It was always surprising to see how quickly the desert swallowed up the airplanes. The planes were always so huge and so noisy as they ripped past us, but in just seconds it seemed, they were sparrows, then dragonflies, and finally mosquitoes. They seemed to shrink away to nothing as they sailed up the canyon and drew nearer to that great rock wall across the river. The rock wall seemed to get bigger and bigger as the plane became smaller and smaller, until finally the little airplane simply disappeared against the dark sandstone.

Flying out over the desert country is risky business. The area is rough, broken, wrinkled and bent. Not the best of places to practice emergency landings. I was fascinated by the story told about the time the Flying Bishop, Bill Wells, was flying out over the desert and a blade on his little plane's propeller simply let go and went spinning off into the wild blue yonder. Metal fatigue, I suppose. The off-balanced prop almost shook the plane to pieces before he could cut the engine. The instrument panel was shaken completely loose and hung down tethered to the firewall by a spaghetti bundle of multi-colored wires and cables. The pilot's feet and rudder pedals were in danger of being entangled in the spilled spaghetti. Not a good thing to have happen at 3000 feet.

Bishop Wells was left sitting in a disabled, dead-stick glider out over the endless rocky crags and canyons. The craters of the moon were rising fast to meet him and it was time to test his angel wings. I'm sure his heart was in his throat and his guts sucked up tight as he steered his disabled lunar lander toward the rocks. He had only one chance, one pass at a flat spot and a split second to decide his fate. If he hesitated too long, the plane would take him down ready or not. He had to drop the nose to maintain airspeed and the ability to control the crash landing, and once he started down he couldn't go back up without stalling. There would be no opportunity for a fly-over to check the field. He scanned the broken canyons ahead as the little plane started to flutter down. He selected a promising spot and cast his fate on the rudder pedal.

In Alaska, much tribute is paid to bush pilots whose skill and daring capture the imagination of many. Bill Wells was as good as any, and probably better than most. He knew the desert and he understood the hazards. He also knew about airplanes. He often landed and took off on dirt strips, farm fields and backcountry roads.

The desert heat rises and wind currents in the canyons are treacherous. The hot rocks and shady canyons create updrafts and downdrafts. Sand dunes and sage bushes grab at airplane wheels before they touch down, and wind-shear might sweep a little craft down into a bottomless canyon like a sheet of discarded paper as it tries to land on a canyon rim. Cedar trees reach out to catch a wingtip, and rocks threaten to rip the belly out if given half a chance. Slickrock is a rough and uneven landing surface, but soft sand will set the plane on its nose. All of these thoughts must have crowded through Bill's mind as the little craft fell from the sky like a wounded Mallard.

God was good to Bishop Wells that day and the spot he selected was doable. The little plane bounced and skipped over rough ground, then shuddered to a stop among the sage bushes. The Eagle had landed.

He had been forced down somewhere on the Burr Desert southeast of Hanksville. No one knew his whereabouts or his situation. He was lucky he was not disabled or killed. He walked many miles across the slickrock and sand flats to a dirt road where he was able to summon help. A few days later he hauled the little plane out on a hay wagon with a team of horses. The plane was repaired and he was back among the eagles in just a week or two. I have often wondered if that wayward propeller blade is sticking in a cedar tree somewhere, and what would some lonesome sheepherder think if he found it there?

From Grandma's house, we could see, way over and across the river, a large boulder above the big ledge that brother Reed always said looked like a hamburger – and it did. It is a massive round and flat rock that stands on edge like a truck tire. There is a vertical crack through the rock, which, with a little imagination, makes it look like a monstrous hamburger bun. The Hamburger Rock was almost due west of Grandma's house. It is still there and I was able to use it as a landmark when I revisited the area many years later in a boat. It can be seen from highway 95 with a pair of binoculars if you look closely.

The Hamburger Rock is above the big ledge on the west side of the Lake. It is on the talus slope, below and to the left of the Wrinkle Rocks, just a little upstream from the mouth of Farley Canyon. The next time you go to the Hite Marina and Lake Powell, say hello to the Hamburger Rock for brother Reed, cousin Janis and me. And, if your boat should stray toward the eastern shore and across the lake from that sandstone marker, take your hat off in respect. You are passing over Grandma's house.

15
The River

The rock walls and the towering sandstone bastions of Glen Canyon are impressive and timeless. The Anasazi would recognize the landmarks as we see them today. In the minds and memories of men, that ocean of stone will endure forever.

Yet, while the sandstone is warm and endearing, it has no soul like a living, moving thing. It was the river that gave Glen Canyon its beating heart. For unlike the rocks and the castle walls, the river was alive and moving.

The mighty Colorado ruled Glen Canyon, and rightfully so. The canyon and all of the red rock country around it was a creation of the river. That endless flow of muddy water, born eons past during forgotten ice ages, forged a path across the western deserts that molded the landscape. Over countless centuries it dug deep into the crust of the earth, carrying the overburden away into the Gulf of California. The rocky channel was scrubbed clean, then tempered strong by the elements.

The river reached out with splayed fingers and drew the desert to her. Numberless little side canyons poured into the river valley in an intricate network of channels like the roots of a tree, fingers spread far and wide, reaching for the distant mountains. The network of canyons formed a lifeline that fed the river with life-giving water.

The river sculpted the canyons from the finest of sandstones, molding the red and brown medium into walls, battlements and castle towers. The water and the wind nibbled at the soft stone for millennia, chewing it down, rasping, buffing, and polishing. The ledges and rock spires towered hundreds of feet above the river channel, sentinels and guardians on the blue-sky horizon. The river burrowed deep into the bedrock, exposing the stark, bleached bones of Mother Earth.

The bones of the earth are the tan and cream-colored sandstones that protrude from the depths wherever erosion has uncovered them. The lighter-colored stone contrasts sharply with the dark reds and browns and adds variety and a change of texture to the sandstone sculptures of the canyons. The off-white rock is harder and denser than the red stone and it has different characteristics. The white stone is smoother and more difficult to walk on, especially for animals with hooves or horses wearing iron shoes. Cowboys have always called it slickrock, and for good reason.

White Canyon

Slickrock erodes differently than the red sandstone. The red stone crumbles, dissolving into smaller and smaller rocks and pebbles until finally becoming coarse red dirt. Slickrock wears down like a bar of soap. It has smooth rounded edges, polished soft by the wind and water.

All across the canyon country there are sheets of slickrock bedded in the dark sandstone like sugar frosting between layers of chocolate cake. White Canyon itself is named for a thick blanket of light-colored stone that melts down into the canyon like a slice of vanilla ice cream left standing on a warm plate.

Slickrock sheds water quickly, and the runoff from summer storms pushes, splashes and inundates the canyon floors in a mad scramble to the river channel. The river always accepted all that was offered, feeding on it and growing strong. The river became braver and bolder as she increased in size and strength, muscling her way down into the shadows of Glen Canyon.

Before Lake Powell, the river was alive and ever changing, and she was at her best in the spring and early summer. During those times of snowmelt and floods, the river was exciting, bold and dangerous. The murky water became thick, dark and red like the blood of dragons. The current was swift and strong. There were swells and troughs like ocean waves in the middle of the river and whole trees were carried past without effort or remorse. The red water ate away at the sandbanks and carelessly drowned the tamaracks and willows. Sometimes the river spilled from its deep channel and spread out over the low-lying areas in the valleys. When the water receded, it left a muddy red band, a bloody bathtub ring as a witness to the level it had crested. At the top of the red-stained high-water mark was a chaff of debris deposited unceremoniously by the receding water: driftwood, sticks, leaves, tumbleweeds and silt.

When the river was high, the town of White Canyon was semi-isolated because all access to the west was severed. The river was dangerous with strong currents and floating debris. The ferryboat surrendered and clung to the safety of the beach, afraid to challenge the angry water. With contempt, the flood washed away the dirt and graveled approaches to the boat landing and scornfully stacked driftwood against the sides of cowering ferryboat.

But in the wintertime, the river was completely different. The infusion of new blood from the side canyons stopped and the Colorado became anemic. The river shrank and retreated to the middle of the channel. Sometimes she looked weak, humble, and almost timid. The red blush was gone from her liquid cheeks. The water turned a cold, dirty gray color during the winter. On each side of the channel, the low water exposed the clean sheets of the river's bed. Long white sandbars spanned the distance between the old high-water line of the tamarack bushes, and the flat, shallow water of winter. The ribbons of sand followed the river as far as the eye could see, white sand shining in the weak winter sunlight. Sometimes there were sandbars in the middle of the river, dividing the flow temporarily into smaller and weaker channels. The low water made the river less dangerous and more accessible.

It was great fun to explore the sandbars along the edge of the river channel. The white sand was as clean as freshly fallen snow. The red dirt had been sifted out and carried away to the blue Pacific. The river dunes were deposited in great, rolling waves and little boys would wallow in the soft depressions before conquering the slopes. The canyon was warm in the wintertime and we could play there without coats most of the time. We would take our shoes off and run and jump and buck in the clean white sand. Little boys enjoyed playing on the sandbars, but we never went there alone. Grandma would not allow us anywhere near the river unless she was there.

The people of the little town sometimes had parties and picnics out on the sandbars. It usually happened in late summer or early fall. The water was low then, and the night air was still warm. People would go to the sandbars in the evenings as the sun sank behind the ledges to the west, and they would build great bonfires of driftwood. They would bring beer and watermelons, picnic baskets, blankets and kids. They would laugh and sing around the fire and have a wonderful time. Those were exciting times for little boys.

Bonfires would light up the river beaches in the night and become glowing beacons that attracted the whole community. Flames would reach high into the desert sky, showering sparks among the stars, red tongues of flame reflecting on the river water far out into the darkness and down the canyon. The huge fire would hiss and pop as soggy driftwood logs swelled and split in the heat. Little boys with happy hearts struggled mightily to feed the hungry fire.

People kicked their shoes off and dug bare toes deep into the clean, warm sand. Beautiful big watermelons, fresh from local gardens, cracked and split open at the very touch of a knife. Beer cans popped and fizzed as pointed steel openers bit through the metal rims of the cans. People laughed and slurped sweet melon juice that ran down their chins and made their arms and hands all sticky. They laughed again as they turned to spit seeds into the shadows, or at passing friends. There were squeals of happy children, the barking of an excited dog, the splash of river water as someone threw a beer bottle, a spent melon rind, or an unsuspecting friend into the shallow water.

White Canyon

Sometimes during the picnics on the river beaches, people would go swimming while others would fish. There were catfish in the river and they were good to eat. Grandpa loved to fish and sometimes he used a trotline to fish the river. A trotline is a long string with several baited hooks attached. It was cast far out into the river by means of a lead weight attached to the end of the string. Grandpa would twirl the lead weight and a few feet of line over his head like a slingshot, then toss it as far as he could out into the channel. The string with the hooks would play out like a kite twine. He would secure the trotline to a strong tamarack bush and leave it in the water for several hours. He would often catch fish for the frying pan.

It was during the recovery of the trotline where I learned the hard way about the physiological differences between catfish and trout. With childish exuberance, I reached out and grabbed a fat catfish as Grandpa was pulling it onto the beach. I got stung pretty good. Colorado River catfish have sharp, defensive spikes in their fins. Grandpa had warned me, but my eagerness overrode my caution … just that one time. Grandma tended my wounds, hugged me until I stopped whimpering, then helped me get even with that smart-alecky catfish. I ate him breaded and sprinkled with lemon, smiling wickedly the whole time.

Men from the mill would sometimes go swimming in the river for recreation and as an antidote for the stifling summer heat. Sometimes a brave soul would swim all the way across the river. It was a life and death wager and few people were up to the challenge. The river had treacherous currents and it was all of four football fields wide between White Canyon and Hite.

Uncle Nate was one of those who could swim the river – and did. Lorraine almost had a coronary one-day when Uncle Var came into the boardinghouse and told her to go look at what her new husband was up to. She saw him sitting on the riverbank on the opposite side of the river, resting before he started back across. That was one of the bad things about swimming the river, you had to do it twice to get back to the starting point. When he swam the river back, Lorraine met her young husband at the edge of the water and scolded him good. She then hugged him, and made him promise to never do it again. I'm sure he never did. He's a man who keeps his promises. I was proud of him when I heard about it, and I told all the kids in school that I had an uncle who could swim the Colorado – and back.

The most famous of the Colorado River swimmers was a man named Claude Simons. Claude had been a Texas Ranger before becoming a uranium prospector, and he was either the bravest or the dumbest man on the desert. Opinions varied.

The story goes, that for some reason, Claude was on the Hite side of the river one sweltering summer afternoon. The White Canyon store with its treasury of beer was on the opposite shore. It had been a long, hot day and Claude was thirsty. He also had a problem. The ferryboat was the only taxi to the beer hall and he would have to pay the fee going each way. It was a potentially costly situation. Beer was the staff of life, no doubt about that, but money was important too. What to do?

And so … Claude did what any self-respecting Texas Ranger would have done under similar circumstances. He swam the river from Hite to White Canyon, bought a case of beer at the store, draped the beer around his neck in a sack, and swam the river back to Hite.

People who saw it said that when he stepped off into the river with his heavy burden of beer, he immediately went under and didn't surface for a long time. They all thought he was a goner. But then, just when they were about to give up on him and go back to the store to have another round of drinks to remember good old Claude, he spouted like a whale, waved happily to his cheering fans, and began a determined breaststroke for the far shore.

In the months and years that followed, whenever people asked him if the story was true, he always smiled and said that the truth of the tale was, he had swam the river with a case and a half of beer – but the half case was in him and not around his neck. He also said he wasn't sure that he'd ever do it again, and not without the extra half case in him, for sure.

Reed and I got to go wading in the mighty Colorado a couple of times, but Grandma, Aunt Lorraine, or Uncle Nate always had us by the wrist in a death-grip. Grandma was afraid of the water and she made me afraid of the water too. It was more fun for little boys to go "swimming" in the big puddles of White Canyon Wash. White Canyon Wash was little-boy tame most of the time, and we could run, jump, splash and play in the mud without an adult clamped to our hand like a coyote trap.

The tributaries that flowed into the river could be dangerous during floods. It was common knowledge among people who lived on the desert country that slickrock sheds water fast, and flash floods are always a threat in the tight, narrow canyons. Grandpa always told us boys to stay out of the slot canyons when it was cloudy. And, if caught in a storm in any of the canyons, we were to wait it out on high ground. Sometimes people were caught in floods miles away from where the rain was falling. A summer storm could happen in the foothills of the Henry Mountains, and miles away in Trachyte or North Wash, the sun would be shining and birds singing when a two or three foot wall of water came crashing down the canyon.

There were many stories of close calls and people who had been caught in the flash floods. For years there was wreckage in North Wash from camp trailers and vehicles that had been caught in flash floods and washed downstream or buried in the mud. Members of our family, on more than one occasion, had to find a high spot in the road and wait for floods to subside in the canyons. Sometimes it was hours before the water would drop enough so the journey could continue. Reed and I waited out a small flood in North Wash with our grandparents one time, but the flood we both remember best was in Iron Wash between Hanksville and Green River.

Tom and Reed McCourt
"Swimming" in White Canyon Wash - 1952

We were on our way to White Canyon, winding through the sage and sand bumps on the dirt road heading for Hanksville. Grandma was waiting for us in White Canyon. It was late '53 or early '54. I was about seven and Reed about five years old. Grandpa had gone to Price for boardinghouse supplies and was taking us back with him.

The River

It had been raining on the San Rafael Swell some miles to the west, and when we got to where the road crosses Iron Wash, we found the channel in full flood. Iron Wash is bigger than most desert washes and it drains an awful lot of country. The wash has a wide, flat bottom and is just a catfish whisker less than a quarter of a mile wide where the road sneaks across it. In those days there was no causeway or culverts in the channel. The road was dirt and it was simply bulldozed across the bottom of the wash.

On that particular day we drove up to the north rim of Iron Wash and found the road ahead underwater. The sun was shining where we were, but it was dark and cloudy to the west. The whole quarter mile of wash bottom was flowing with muddy water.

Grandpa cussed and growled a little. He was anxious to get back home to White Canyon. He had uranium to find and he didn't have time for stupid floods. He walked down the embankment to where the water licked at the road in the bottom of the wash. He then stuck a stick in the dirt at the edge of the water. He rolled a cigarette and waited impatiently, tapping his toe, his frustrations going up in smoke. He stood with his arms folded and his back straight, his feet planted solidly. He looked out across that muddy water with eyes squinted and his jaw set. He looked like Moses, about to raise his arms and rebuke the offending flood.

Presently, he pronounced that the water was dropping. There was almost an inch of wet sand between his stick and the turbid water. We waited for another hour or so, and the water moved back from the stick another four to six inches. We boys played in the sand dunes, chased lizards, and generally had a good time. Grandpa huffed and puffed on his cigarettes, sending smoke signals down the draw. He had a dozen cigarette butts stomped dead at his feet and a wide semi-circle of boot tracks beaten into the sand at the edge of the water. His tracks looked like the spot where the dog hits the end of the chain.

Finally, Grandpa raised the hood on the little pickup truck, and with a wrench he took the fan belt off. He explained to us that when you cross deep water in a vehicle it is necessary to disable the fan so it doesn't throw water on the spark plugs and distributor. Water will stall the engine. He explained to us that while the wash was wide, it was relatively flat-bottomed. The floodwater stretched far toward the opposite shore, but he didn't think it was more than about a foot deep anywhere in the channel.

He stuffed us kids in the truck and told us to hang on tight. He started the engine and eased the little rig out into the edge of the water. He had to hurry. Without the fan belt, the engine would soon overheat.

White Canyon

That Jeep truck was one of those anemic little outfits from the 1940s. It had a flat-head, four-cylinder engine that couldn't pull your hat off. A few years later, Grandpa bought a brand new 1957 Chevy pickup with a more powerful six-cylinder engine. But on the day we challenged Iron Wash, we were in the little Jeep.

Grandpa nosed the truck into the flood cautiously, and then he stood on the accelerator. Almost immediately, muddy water was splashing over the hood and blotting the windshield. Thankfully, the little truck was four-wheel drive and she gave us all she had. She bucked, bounced and splashed through the flood, as first the front wheels, and then the back wheels, caught something to hold on to. The truck screamed and spit and sputtered while the windshield wipers struggled mightily to keep up. Steam swirled from under the hood. I don't remember if he had a tailpipe extension to get the exhaust up and out of the water or not, but he must have done something because the engine never stalled even though the water came up and over the bumpers.

The front bumper was pushing water like the prow of a boat. Water came bubbling up through the floorboards and around the doors. Water washed over our feet and legs. We boys pulled our legs up onto the seat to try to keep from getting wet. We held on to the seat, the dashboard, the door, and each other, trying to keep from being bucked off the seat. Grandpa had his teeth clenched tight and his lips drawn back in a snarl. He had both hands on the steering wheel and his foot heavy on the accelerator. Water splashed and swirled around his boots.

We could feel the truck sliding sideways in the current. Grandpa steered frantically with both hands, trying to keep her pointed at the dirt road on the far shore. There were no delineator posts or guardrails to outline the course of the road. He kept his foot heavy on the gas pedal while the little truck roared, splashed, kicked like a frog and dog-paddled valiantly.

It was terribly exciting, but scary, too. It was very much like being in Grandpa's motorboat out in the middle of the Colorado with nothing but moving water all around.

Finally, and just in the nick of time, the deep water dropped away suddenly and the little truck caught solid footing with all four feet. She lunged for the far shore and stomped and splashed that last forty yards before dragging herself up on dry ground on the other side of the wash.

Grandpa hurried to turn the engine off. The truck was overheating and steam was boiling from under the hood with a loud hiss, cold water sizzling on hot metal. As we opened the doors to get out, water rushed from across the floorboards and from under the seats and splashed on the ground, making a large, dark stain in the sand.

We boys stood looking back at that wide expanse of moving water and we started to laugh and jump up and down. We were excited and thrilled by the adventure. Grandpa looked just a little sheepish and admitted that the water was just a little deeper than he had expected.

Grandpa peeled back the tarp over the back of the truck and inspected and rearranged the boxes of groceries. He then lifted the hood of the truck, reinserted the fan belt, and we continued our journey toward Hanksville. Grandpa's boots and pant legs were wet, almost to his knees, but he seemed not to notice.

When we told Grandma about our adventure late that evening, she was so interested that she asked us all about the exciting details. She then gave Grandpa one of those cold, "I'll get you later" type of looks. Grandpa tried to laugh and wave it off. He said something to her like, "Oh hell, Bertha, it wasn't that bad … you know how kids are!" Those little boys never forgot that wild ride in the muddy water of Iron Wash. I don't think that old man did either.

Like the flood washes, the river could be treacherous and cruel. She claimed a few lives when we were there. There is a story about some children at White Canyon playing near the river. They came running back to their parents and told of seeing a "black man" floating down the river. Some adults went to the river with the kids to check it out, but the black man was gone. He had drifted on down the canyon. No one had been reported missing that anyone knew about, and since the eyewitnesses were just kids, no alarm was sounded and no search ever conducted that I am aware of.

I've always thought the report the kids made was probably credible, especially since they described the body as being a black man. Any body in the water long enough to float, even a caucasian, would look very dark. I've wondered for years who that "black man" in the river might have been.

In about 1960, a man named Reed Maxfield was running Arth Chaffin's ferryboat. He had a wife and kids and a bright future in front of him. But one day the river took him. It was an accident. When he fell into the river, the muddy water closed over him. His body was found two weeks later at the Glen Canyon dam site in Arizona.

There was another drowning at the Hite ferry site that affected me deeply. The drowning victim was just a kid, nine years old. His name was Johnny Marsing. I was two years younger, but I knew Johnny Marsing. I didn't know him well, but I had met him and played in the dirt with him and the Seager kids one long summer afternoon.

In June 1953 a group of White Canyon residents were joyriding in a motorboat. They passed the ferry site on their way down the river. At the ferry site, the long metal cables hung suspended just above the river. At high water time, the cables hung so low they sometimes slapped in the water as the ferryboat tugged on them. The people in the boat passed under those low-hanging cables and forgot that Johnny was sitting on the prow of the boat. He was sitting with his legs hanging over the front of the boat, holding on to the anchor ring like a rodeo cowboy. He had no place to go as the steel cables came at him. The cables ripped him from the boat and slapped him out into the river. He was not wearing a life vest.

They turned the boat around as quickly as possible and went back for him. His father saw him in the water, and said he was trying to swim and reaching out for help. But before they got to him, the current pulled him under. His body was never found.

Uncle Nate and other men from the mill went down the river in boats. They searched for twelve miles, to the mouth of Red Canyon. For two days they swam in the shallows and searched the rocks, driftwood snags, sandbanks and willows in the hope that Johnny might have beaten the river and crawled to shore somewhere. They even hoped to find his body on a snag or in an eddy. The men came back badly sunburned, discouraged, beaten, and completely worn out. Bill Wells flew the river back and forth, searching from the air, but the river never gave him back.

The drowning of Johnny Marsing was a heavy blow to me. It was the first time I truly became aware that young people could die. Before that time, only old people died. It made me afraid. Life wasn't fair when kids like Johnny Marsing died too. It was scary.

When I hit bottom, and cried, and was much distressed about it all, Grandma talked to me about it. She told me it didn't matter if they never found his body. He wasn't in that muddy water any more, and he wasn't in that dead body anymore either. God had taken him from the river and he was in heaven now. She promised me that I would see him again some day, and she promised me he would be healthy and happy and he would have a new body. She told me that his new body would look just like his old one, God would be sure of that. I stopped crying. I hugged my Grandma. And I was happy again.

I believed her then, and I believe her now. But I've never crossed that river or Lake Powell since that day without looking into the dark water and thinking about Johnny Marsing, my boyhood friend, who went to live with

The River

God in heaven, and left his old body in the river. [1]

My family too had a very close call with the river. Aunt Lorraine almost lost her precious, oldest son to the dark water in early 1954. Cousin Winn was about eighteen months old when he wandered away from his mother and found his way to the riverbank. Lorraine and Nate were living on the north side of White Canyon Wash at the time, and the muddy Colorado rolled past just a little to the west of them. It took only a moment of mother's distraction to allow the adventurous toddler to find his way to the river.

He couldn't have been gone for more than a few minutes, but when Lorraine missed him, and started to search, she spotted him standing on the riverbank near the water. It was springtime and the river was high. The sandbank he was standing on stood a couple of feet above the water and it had been undercut by the moving current. The baby stood teetering on the edge, innocently throwing handfuls of dirt at the passing water.

She didn't want to startle him by screaming or yelling at him to come back, so she moved quickly and on the wings of angels and scooped him up from behind before he knew she was there. The baby's feet came off the ground and the sandbank went into the water in a single motion. The collapsing riverbank almost got her and the baby too, but she was able to step back and regain her balance.

Of course she went to pieces. She cried and hugged that fat little rascal and thanked God for their deliverance. Grandpa was so shook up when he heard about it that he took his little D-4 caterpillar and made a steep wall of red dirt between the cabin and the river. The baby lived in the shadow of a hawk for a long time after that.

The Colorado could be dangerous, but she was beneficial as well. She was also beautiful. I wish I could have seen her the way John Wesley Powell and that first batch of river runners saw her in 1869 and 1872. Before there were dams and irrigation projects upstream, the river in Glen Canyon would have been much larger. There were no tamarack bushes back then and the riverbanks would have been covered with native willow and cottonwood.

I've always thought it a cruel joke that Lake Powell was named after the man who discovered and loved Glen Canyon. John Wesley Powell stood in awe of the river and the canyons. He was a man who treasured the majesty and the beauty of the place. He gave Glen Canyon and the river glowing praise in his journals, speeches and reports. How thoughtless to attach his name to the thing that killed them.

The lake should have been named after the politicians who willed it there, those who could have stopped it if only they had tried. The dead water should have been named Lake Eisenhower, or Lake Goldwater.

I was just a little kid when I first heard they were going to damn the river (pun intended). I remember Grandpa pointing up to the ledges around his home and telling us the water would be two hundred feet deep right there where the house was. I remember asking him if we could still visit the old Indian fort in his motorboat, and him telling me no, it would all be underwater. I just couldn't believe it.

For years I really didn't think it could happen. I didn't think they could overcome that river. I knew they were working on the Glen Canyon Dam, but I didn't think the river could be stopped.

I knew that river. I had crossed it in a motorboat and I had crossed it on Arth Chaffin's ferry. I had seen it spill from it's deep channel and eat away the sandbanks and tamaracks. I had watched it carry whole cottonwood trees, effortlessly, down the canyon. I had marveled at how wide and deep and strong it was. I had felt its strength and power. I had witnessed its unwavering resolve to push through that river canyon.

And while I stood in reverent awe of the muscle and the majesty of the mighty Colorado, at the same time, she was my friend. I had played along her muddy banks and I had waded in her shoals. I had frolicked across her sandbars and ate catfish from her depths. She had playfully swallowed the pebbles I had thrown out to her, gulping them down with polite, little-boy-sized splashes. She had perfumed the air around my grandmother's home and happily tossed about the little stick-boats I had cast into her lap. She had taken the imaginary little boats with her on her journey through the canyons, a memento of our special time together.

That river was one of God's greatest creations. She had carved the canyons, sculpted the sandstone and molded the landscape for a million years. Her vast tons of muddy water pushed down the river canyon like a great battering ram. I didn't think she could be stopped. I fully expected that when that steel and concrete monument to man's haughty presumption was put to the test, the river would simply push through it and continue on her way as she had always done.

Sadly, I was wrong.

Notes:

1. Johnny Marsing, the young boy who drowned in the river, is in the group photo of White Canyon school children on page 49.

16
A trip to Red Canyon

I don't remember which year it was, 1957 or 1958, but Grandpa took brother Reed and me on a trip to Red Canyon. He was going to Red Canyon to do assessment work on uranium claims. My grandparents had left the desert by then, and they had been working for the city of Sunnyside at the pump house in Range Creek, pumping water over the mountain. I was eleven or twelve at that time. Reed would have been nine or ten.

Even though he had moved off the desert, Grandpa kept up the annual assessment work on his uranium claims. He held some potentially valuable properties and he fulfilled his legal obligations. He still had hope the feds would do the right thing and buy his holdings before the lake drowned some of them and cut access to the others.

Like Arth Chaffin, he and the Southern Cross Uranium Company fought a David and Goliath battle with the federal government until the mid-1960s. And like Arth Chaffin, Grandpa and Southern Cross ended up with only legal bills for their trouble. Uranium was no longer the apple of Uncle Sam's eye. The construction of the Glen Canyon dam and Lake Powell was now at the top of the federal agenda. Those brave sons who had answered the call and discovered the Atomic Monster's hiding places were not needed any longer. They and their mining claims were impediments now to the inundation of Glen Canyon. In the years to come, dozens of prospectors and miners would watch the water cover their hard-won gains while the government sold them down the river in the federal courts.

Red Canyon was downriver from White Canyon about twelve miles. But to get there in a pickup truck, a person had to go clear back to the rim of Grand Gulch toward Blanding and drive around the Red Rock Plateau. To gain those twelve miles, it was necessary to drive almost eighty miles, and the road was an adventure in those days.

So, when we left Wellington to go to Red Canyon, instead of going through Hanksville, Hite and White Canyon, we went the long way around through Moab and Blanding. The trip was about fifty miles longer going that way, but there were many more miles of pavement and we didn't have to pay the ferryboat fee.

We crossed the Colorado River at Moab on the old river bridge and stopped in town for Gas. Moab was touted as "The Uranium Capitol of the World," but she looked more like a typical Utah farm town to me. Of course there was a brand new uranium mill in town, and several new homes and businesses. There were lots of camp trailers down by the river, and every sign in town had the words "Atomic" or "Uranium" shouting from the stencils. But if you looked behind the façade, Moab was still wearing the overalls and straw hat of her agricultural founders. There were always farmers and cowboys in town, and beat up old pickup trucks with bales of hay and ugly dogs in the back. Horses and cows lounged in dusty pastures right in the middle of town, and wide, empty hay fields followed the creek up Spanish Valley.

A lot of people still made a living in the mining industry in '57 and '58, but the wild and mad-dash days of the uranium boom were over. Things were more settled and organized now. The Atomic Monster had been found and was now the property of multi-national corporations. Big companies with proper credentials and important sounding names were paying Navajos and the sons of Mormon farmers to disembowel the Monster deep in the earth and drag his guts out into the sunshine. For their efforts, the miners were getting three dollars an hour and lethal doses of radon gas. But none of them knew it yet.

Mining was good for the local tax base and Moab's citizens reveled in her radioactive notoriety. The mining industry wouldn't cave in for another few years and the town was fat and happy. The tourist explosion hadn't happened yet, and no one had ever heard of a mountain bike.

Moab was a humble community of farmhouses, country stores, camp trailers and a couple of poor-boy motels back then, but there was one grand castle in town. It was a huge home perched high on the side of a hill that looked down on all the little people. It was the Eagle's Nest of Charles Augustus Steen, the desert Sultan of southern Utah. Steen was the man who discovered the legendary Mi Vida (My Life) mine that made him a multi-millionaire in the early days of the uranium boom. His story is fascinating because it packaged all of the elements driving the uranium boom into one man's story. The dream, the struggle, the glory and the heartbreak, are all chapters of the Charlie Steen saga.

Charlie Steen was born in Texas and educated at the Texas College of Mines. He graduated in 1943 with a B.S. degree in Geology. Poor eyesight had kept him out of the military during World War II. After graduation, the new geologist worked the Texas oil patch for a while, but a freewheeling nature and a mind-of-his-own often got him into trouble with supervisors and corporate big wigs.

A trip to Red Canyon

In December, 1949 he was out of work and down on his luck. In one of his geology periodicals, he read an article about the government's quest for radioactive treasure on the Utah frontier. Charlie was instantly smitten. If grocery clerks and railroad bums could find uranium in the four corners area, surely he, a trained geologist, could run the Atomic Monster to ground. He decided to emigrate to Utah, find the treasure and fulfill his destiny. His mother gave him a thousand dollar grubstake to help him on his way.

Charlie had a wife and four young sons, and he took them with him to Utah. For two years they lived as poor as church mice. They lived in a tarpaper shack in the tiny tumbleweed town of Cisco, out on the bleak and windswept sand flats north of Moab. Things were tough and Charlie often poached deer to help feed his family.

Unlike most prospectors who trolled the surface with Geiger counters, Charlie had a plan. He had studied the geology of the area, and he was casting his fate on a hunch. He suspected the Monster was hiding deep and he worked a decrepit old drilling rig, probing the depths to find out. Every cent he could scrape together was invested in gas and drilling equipment.

"Government experts" said he was wasting his time in that particular area. Everyone knew the Atomic Monster was hiding further south near the four corners. But Charlie was from Texas and he had a hard head. The government experts were geologists and he was a member of the club. He knew enough about geology to suspect that the experts probably didn't know what they were talking about. Less educated prospectors, and those who trusted government experts, went further south to search.

Then, in July 1952, Charlie drilled through the belly of the Atomic Monster as it lay hidden deep in Lisbon Valley southeast of Moab. In the first six months of production he shipped a million dollars worth of uranium ore assaying up to 87 percent pure. At that time it was the largest single deposit of high-grade uranium ore found in the United States.

Within a few months, Charlie and his family went from subsistence soda crackers to flying a private plane to Salt Lake City once a week for rumba lessons. He built his Eagle's Nest home on the hill east of Moab for the ungodly sum of $250,000 dollars. He threw parties for the whole community that were the talk of the town for years. He had his old, worn-out work boots bronzed, and he was elected to the Utah state senate in 1958.

Charlie Steen was generous, kind and compassionate. When the money came pouring in, he remembered his old friends and people who had helped him when he was down and out. In Moab he donated many acres of land and many thousands of dollars to community projects and worthy causes.

White Canyon

The people of Moab loved him because he preferred to be one of them. He stayed in southern Utah among his old friends and acquaintances while most others who made a little money in the uranium business ran off to the comforts of the big city. The man was a legend in his own time. Everyone who bought a Geiger counter in the mid-1950s dreamed of striking it rich like Charlie Steen.

For a few years, Charlie was the most famous and most sought-after man on the desert. He became Utah's favorite adopted native son. He started several companies and everything he touched turned to gold. He built and owned the uranium-processing mill in Moab that was later sold to Atlas Minerals.

Charlie basked in the radioactive limelight for a while, but slowly he became disillusioned with The Great State of Utah. The state tax people picked his pockets and hovered over everything he did like circling buzzards. It all came to a head in 1961 when a bill he was sponsoring through the Utah senate to allow Utahans to buy liquor by the drink was shot down. In disgust, Charlie resigned from the Utah Senate and moved his family and his money to Nevada. His Eagle Nest house on the hill in Moab is a restaurant now - The Sunset Grill.

In Nevada, Charlie could buy liquor by the drink, and Nevada had no state income taxes and fewer state revenue buzzards. He built a grand mansion on a ranch south of Reno. The hilltop castle in the pines was made of native stone and the domed and gabled roof was all copper. The new and improved Eagle's Nest spanned 22,000 square feet (that's more than half-an-acre) and the dooryard was eight thousand acres of Washoe Valley ranch.

Charlie's castle had a massive reception hall and a grand dining room surrounded by an indoor moat (cross my heart). The indoor swimming pool was forty feet long and nineteen feet deep. There was a magnificent, freestanding fireplace and a huge patio with an electric, rollaway roof. Steen is said to have paid over one million 1962 dollars for his new digs – not counting the land, of course.

It was a castle custom-made for "The King of Uranium," but his Lordship didn't enjoy it for long. It's a sad story to tell, but while Charlie had great ability for finding uranium, all the money he made slipped through his fingers. He "diversified" his interests and sent truckloads of money down roads he didn't know, horse breeding and aircraft production to name only a couple. By 1968 he was broke.

He was calling in his markers and trying to refinance and reorganize his ventures when the feds pounced on his misfortunes. They seized his properties for back taxes, beat the hell out of him in court, humiliated him good in the press, and turned him out into the cold, cruel world, broke but not broken. He immediately went back to the desert and started the search all over again. If he could do it once, he could do it twice. But sadly, Charlie died broke before finding another pot of gold.

Like Robin Hood, Charlie Steen is still a hero to many of the old timers in Grand and San Juan Counties. He was a common man who sprouted strong from humble roots. He was a man of imagination and true grit, a free spirit who would not be fettered. Once he fed his hungry family with deer poached from the king's forest, then, for a while, he took buckets of money from the rich and powerful federal government and shared some of it with his friends. It was a great party while it lasted.

As we continued our journey south of Moab, that narrow little strap of paved highway stretched into the high desert toward Monticello and Blanding. The snow-capped La Sal Mountains loomed off to the left and presently the crown of the Blue Mountain could be seen to the right.

As the road approached the little town of Monticello, it began to skirt great, sculptured fields that stretched out to the south and east for miles and miles. They are beautiful and colorfully textured fields of grain, beans and grass. They are dry farms, fields without ditches and canals, an anomaly in most of Utah. To farmers who toil mightily to bring mountain water to desert fields, dry farming is like cheating. In most of Utah, flood irrigation is half the work of farming. Farmers around Monticello, Blanding and Dove Creek, Colorado are blessed. God loves them and sends water from the sky.

Our next stop was in Blanding, one of the best little towns in all the world. Blanding was another of those small Mormon pioneer outposts born in the vastness of the Utah desert. For many years it had struggled toward prosperity in near isolation. The people were friendly and the little town always looked neat and orderly to me. Around the town were beautiful fields and farms. To the north, the Blue Mountain, sometimes called the Abajos, stood tall and friendly. To the south and east, the high desert fell away toward the Four Corners, Shiprock and Mesa Verde. The town was on the edge of the Navajo lands and there were always colorfully dressed Indians on the sidewalks and in the stores.

Blanding is the gateway to Cedar Mesa and the Glen Canyon country. In those days, the road to White Canyon and Hite left town to the west and struck out bravely toward the heights of Elk ridge. That dirt road was the lifeline to White Canyon, Natural Bridges National Monument, Grand

Gulch, and points south. The Comb Ridge that stretched her unyielding spine the many miles between Blanding and Bluff had been breached by a single track by then, but it was a narrow and dangerous road. It clawed up the west face of the ridge, squeezed through a crack in the sandstone, then spilled into Butler Wash. The long, steep dugway was wide enough for only one vehicle. If another truck was encountered, someone had to back up. The Comb Wash road was a poor second choice, and my family used it most in winter when the Elk Ridge road was closed by snow. Utah's famous bicentennial highway, U95, would one day follow that same trail up and through Comb Ridge, but it wouldn't be built for another twenty years.

The Elk Ridge road climbed the east face of the mountain. It clawed through ravines, teetered on narrow, rocky ridges, and pushed through thick brush and boulders, finally finding its way to the high country where it broke out into a world of pine and quaking aspen.

Elk Ridge is beautiful mountain country in the midst of the desert and most people don't know it is there. From the distant highways in the valleys, it looks like any other high desert escarpment, but up close and personal, it's a national forest. It has one serious shortcoming. There is no running water. No high mountain streams, lakes or fishponds of any kind.

The most prominent terrain feature on Elk ridge is called The Bears Ears. From the south, looking north across the desert from places like the Utah-Arizona state line in Monument Valley, the Bears Ears can be seen from more than 50-miles away. And with just a little imagination, the two rocky points do look like the top of a big old bear's head with his rounded ears protruding into the sky. The Bears Ears are the highest points on Elk Ridge and exceed 9,000 feet in elevation. From a distance they are dark and covered with fur, but as they get closer they become soft red sandstone.

When I was a kid, I truly loved going to and from White Canyon through Blanding because we got to go over the Bears Ears. There was something inherently wicked and delightful about bumping a pickup truck over the top of that old bear's head. As we approached Elk Ridge from White Canyon, we boys would sit on the very edge of the truck seat and gape hard at the mountains ahead for that first enchanting glimpse of the Bears Ears. And when we finally saw them we would squeal with delight.

I remember one trip in particular. It was 1952 and Reed and I were traveling with Aunt Lorraine and Uncle Nate. Lorraine didn't have any kids of her own yet, but she loved kids and delighted in teasing and playing with us. We were props for her motherhood training, and she experimented and practiced all sorts of mothering skills and nurturing tortures on us.

A trip to Red Canyon

Lucky for us, she was to get her own little boy later that same year, and she cuddled, teased, and played with him like a cat with a mouse. She named him Winn Noyes, and he grew up to be an Army Colonel and as tough as nails. The poor kid had to be tough to survive his mother's loving torments.

Aunt Lorraine knew the charm the Bears Ears held for little boys, and on that 1952 trip she had us worked into a frenzy before the mountain even came in sight. She would sigh wistfully and clasp her hands together dramatically like a soap-opera TV star, and say something like, "I wonder what that old bear is up to today? Do you think he'll get us this time Nate? Do you really think it's safe for us to drive across his ears?"

Uncle Nate would grin and say, "I don't know for sure, but I think we can make it if we hurry right along. It's still morning and that old bear might still be sleeping."

The anticipation nearly killed us. Reed and I were both wiggling around on the truck seat like we were going to wet ourselves. Lorraine giggled like a schoolgirl.

The Bears Ears – Author photo

Finally, the Bears Ears were in sight and Uncle Nate said we'd just give it our best shot and hope for the best. At the base of the mountain he shifted down as the little truck dug in and started to climb the steep rocky dugway that took us to the Bears Ears. We boys held our breath and peeked out over the dashboard with big eyes and trembling excitement. Aunt Lorraine smiled and stage-whispered to Uncle Nate that we'd better be careful and lock the doors. The little truck crested the dugway and inched its way through the thick cedar trees and right up and over the old bear's ears.

It's always a shock to crest the Bears Ears from the south. You travel for miles in red sand, red rocks, cedar trees and sage bushes, and then suddenly the whole world changes. You top that steep ridge and drive between the Bears Ears and the world suddenly falls away on the north side. There before you spreads a beautiful mountain meadow of tall grass, quaking aspen, royal pines and cool, clean air. The desert has suddenly disappeared. It's like passing through a door into another world. The desert is behind you and the forest in front of you.

Uncle Nate stopped the truck right on the crest of the Bears Ears. There was a towering bastion of shattered red sandstone on either side of us, the ears of the bear. The red desert and Grand Gulch stretched far away to the south. A high mountain meadow lay at our feet to the north.

Uncle Nate smiled and said that we'd made it. The old bear couldn't get us now. We got out of the truck to make a nature call and admire the view. I delighted in peeing on the old bear's head. I jumped up and down to wake him up and see how he liked it.

On our trip to Red Canyon with Grandpa a few years later, we stopped on the Bears Ears again. It was a great place for a rest stop. It is the highest point on the mountain and the views are long and spectacular. Grandpa pointed out the Henry Mountains to the west and Navajo Mountain to the South. From the Bears Ears, Navajo Mountain is a great rounded dome, a magnificent Hogan of a mountain that slumbers in the heat shimmer far to the south in Arizona. Grandpa explained that the San Juan River ran in front of Navajo Mountain and joined the Colorado somewhere off to the south and west. Grand Gulch was a great crack in the sandstone just below us. It too disappeared in the haze somewhere to the south.

The country was empty. I don't remember seeing another person during that three-day trip. The uranium boom was unofficially over and the prospectors and miners had retreated back to town, humbled and beaten. The mining camps lay empty as a warm desert breeze sprinkled sand in the caterpillar tracks. The desert was beginning the healing process. In the coming years, raindrops and wind would scrub the desert floor, while bunchgrass and sage did their very best to bandage wounds on the mesas.

There was a feeling in the air back then, a feeling of true isolation that isn't there anymore. It was the feeling of knowing that you really were all alone. It was an era before cell phones and CB radios and the desert simply swallowed you up. The desert closed behind you like a door. You were on your own and out-of-touch, come what may. I'm sure we had many of the same feelings old-time sailors had when they set out on the world's oceans in little wooden ships.

We sailed out into that ocean of wilderness, dropping off the Bears Ears and following the steep and winding road to the foot of the mountain and Grand Flat, the very head of Grand Gulch. Cedar Mesa and Grand Gulch were on our left. Natural Bridges National Monument on our right. Even Natural Bridges was empty. There were no tourists, no visitor center, no rangers, no restrooms and no tollbooth. The place didn't have a full-time park service presence in those days.

We drove past the Natural Bridges many times when I was a kid and we never did stop to see them. The whole country was a scenic wonderland. It seemed almost silly that someone in Washington had designated one small corner of it as a scenic wonder. I didn't see the Natural Bridges until the late 1980s. By then I was more than forty years old and went there as a leader for a troop of brain-dead Boy Scouts. But then, that's another story (wink).

We dropped off the Bears Ears and continued our journey through a forest of pinion and juniper to a fork in the road in the shadow of Moss Back Butte. If we had taken the right-hand fork we could have gone to White Canyon and Hite. We took instead the left fork, the road less traveled, and struck out across the sand flats toward Hall's Crossing and Red Canyon.

That road less traveled is a paved highway now, U-276. Sounds like a German submarine doesn't it? The road follows very close to the same route taken by the Hole In The Rock pioneers in 1880. The road begins at Harmony Flat, parallels the Red House Cliffs, climbs the fabled Clay Hill Divide and skirts just a little north of Grey Mesa.

The road ends today at the Hall's Crossing Marina on Lake Powell. When we followed the road in the late 1950s, it was still just a dirt track that petered-out somewhere on the Glen Canyon Rim. It was a road to and from nowhere and it was always empty. The wind quickly rubbed-out tire tracks in the sand, and the road always looked and felt like there was no one out there ahead of you. It is amazing how something as simple as that will dramatically increase a person's feeling of isolation.

White Canyon

We followed the empty road south for twelve or fifteen miles into the desert. From high atop the Moss Back Butte, that little '57 Chevrolet must have looked like a tiny beetle crawling across the clean desert sand far below. In front of it, the sand was clean and smooth and unmarred by any blemish. Behind it, a long trail of scuffmarks, little Chevrolet beetle tracks, stretched back toward Elk Ridge. The desert wind had work to do.

Down the road we turned off to the right where an even more primitive and dusty little cow track of a jeep trail squeezed through a gap in the Red House cliffs. Soon we were at the head of Red Canyon.

The Red Canyon road is a long, stark, bleak and depressing scratch on the earth's surface, even today. After traveling through places like White Canyon, Elk Ridge and Cedar Mesa, there is absolutely nothing of interest in Red Canyon. It is a rough and rocky moonscape, the backside of the red planet Mars. The towering Tables Of The Sun can be seen to the north, butting up against the Moss Back Butte, but the rest of it is nothing but rocks, red dirt and sand. And to make matters worse, the road fell away forever down that rough and dusty track. It was all of thirty miles from the Red House Cliffs to the river, maybe more. The road teetered on the edge of a barren, deep, ugly desert gulch for most of the way.

It was late fall, probably November, and darkness overtook us near the head of Red Canyon. We stopped for the night near the crest of the watershed in a thin clump of cedar trees where we could make a campfire. It was getting cold. A chilling wind swept sand toward the east.

Grandpa dug a fire pit and kindled a fire while we boys scavenged for wood. Then we ate fried potatoes and pork and beans hot from the skillet. The sun sank into a dark cloudbank far to the west and the wind increased with the growing darkness.

The wind tugged at our straw hats and sent cold, icy fingers up our pant legs as we sat on the ground by the fire. The stiff breeze seasoned our food with wind-borne ashes and sand. The wind slapped flames over the edge of the fire pit, causing the fire to pop and hiss. Bright showers of sparks rode away on the wind, then winked out like popping bubbles as the cold air stole the heat. Pinion knots glowed brightly in the fire pit like coals in a blacksmith's forge, fanned by a bellows.

We turned our collars up and sucked our heads deep into our coats. We pulled our hats down tight and tucked our pant legs around the tops of our boots. We ate our meal all humped over, arms and legs tucked in close to our bodies, feet close to the fire.

A trip to Red Canyon

We rolled out our beds as the darkness gathered. We slept in the back of the pickup where we would be up and out of the blowing sand. We took advantage of the thin metal truck bed as a windbreak. Grandpa never used a tent. The three of us were crowded there, but warm. Grandpa knew how to camp on the desert. He had a cotton mattress that filled the bed of the truck, plenty of blankets and a big canvas tarp to wrap everything up in.

It was dark and scary that night. No moon, and the cold wind whistled and whispered endlessly through the bed of the truck. We were snug in our mound of blankets, but we had a deep feeling of apprehension. No one said anything, but we could all feel it.

We knew there might be a big storm coming, and that was scary, but there was something else, too. There was something eerie about the tortured squeal of the wind. I pulled the quilts up tight around my face, and I noticed that grandpa had his pistol near his pillow. He could feel the uneasiness too. Something was out there somewhere, and I was glad I was with Grandpa, and glad he had a gun.

We were camped on a high desert ridge that night, but as far as we could see in any direction there was not a light. There was also not a sound, other than the wind. It was like camping on the moon. I could peek out from my warm blankets and make out the top of the distant ledges by where the dim stars ended. I lay awake for a long time watching cold, faraway planets shimmer like ice crystals in the winter sky. Meteors zipping through the darkness like tiny snowballs.

We were alone, and the vast, dark emptiness squeezed in around us. The bed of the pickup truck was a lifeboat on an ocean of nothingness. There, in that Chevrolet lifeboat was the warmth of life, an ark of humanity filled with hopes, fears and dreams. Human consciousness reached out timidly and tested the wind and the darkness, analyzing the signals, summing up the possibilities, calculating the odds and planning defensive strategies. Outside of those low metal walls, the empty lifelessness stretched out forever into the darkness. The cold wind moaned and cried.

When the endless night finally ended, Grandpa stoked up the campfire and cooked us breakfast. The cold wind went away with the darkness and the sun came up warm and alive. The ice crystal stars melted into a blue morning sky as the sun reached out to touch them. The morning sun chased the shadows away and kissed me warmly on the cheek. She warmed my clothes and warmed my heart and gave me joy and courage.

The desert was completely different in the new morning light. The phantoms and ghouls that had stalked us during the night were gone. The bright sun swept all fear and apprehension away. Flat, featureless shadows retreated and the vibrant colors and textures of the desert came back warm and friendly. To the east, the air was hazy in the golden shimmer of the sunrise. The red, brown and gold of the desert floor met sunbeams in the air to form a mist of glowing radiance. Storm clouds that had threatened us the night before had disappeared.

After breakfast we continued our journey into the depths of Red Canyon. It was my first and only trip there. We followed the tortured, narrow road as it teetered drunkenly along the edge of the deep wash. We went down, down, into that deep canyon of shattered red rocks and sterile red sand that gave the place its name.

Near the mouth of Red Canyon, the road dropped into the very bottom of the sandy wash. It was the only flat and level place available. We could finally see where the Colorado River was, even though we couldn't see the water yet. Red Canyon was finally opening up, losing her identity and becoming part of Glen Canyon.

We were winding down the sandy wash when I looked up and saw a perfectly square doorway peeking from the shadows of an overhanging ledge. The image was there for just a second and then gone. "There's a cliff house!" I shouted excitedly. Grandpa, who had been in the canyon dozens of times and spent many weeks there working uranium claims, looked at me like I was crazy. He said there weren't any cliff houses in Red Canyon that he knew about. "Oh yes there is!" I said confidently "I saw it. Let's go back and climb up to it!" Grandpa didn't believe me. He said we were going to stop and camp soon. Maybe Reed and I could go back and look for it later.

I was bitterly disappointed. I was an imaginative little buck to be sure, and I often chased butterflies of fancy somewhere over the rainbow. Grandpa knew that, and he didn't want to start down the yellow brick road with me. I had earned his skepticism. But at the same time, I knew the cliff house was there. God painted the wilderness with curved and wavy lines. Only a man would make a perfectly square doorway deep in the ledges.

Just a few hundred yards more and we drove out of the wash and into the sunshine of Glen Canyon. The muddy Colorado smiled as she rolled past. We parked near the river where the skeletons of a few empty old buildings drooped sadly, the remains of an abandoned uranium camp. Grandpa said we would stay there for the night. He pointed hopefully at the river and some big sand hills nearby, but I was so excited about the little square doorway I didn't care about anything else. Grandpa finally shook his head in a resigned, suffering sort of way, and told us we could go back and check it out if we wanted to.

Brother Reed and I half-walked and half-ran back up that narrow wash following Chevrolet tracks in the sand as we searched for that elusive doorway in the rocks. The magic door was well hidden and it took a while to find it again. I grew anxious and desperate, but I was determined. Finally, I caught that little doorway out in the open again. With a squeal of excitement we clambered up the rocks to see what was there.

There was actually a cave there, a deep overhanging ledge in the rocks that could not be seen from the wash below. In the cave was a beautiful Anasazi ruin. I wanted to throw my head back and howl like a coyote.

The doorway was centered in a granary-type structure that sat next to a large, semi-subterranean room. The large room was sunk down into the dirt of the cave floor like a Kiva. The mud and rock walls of the "D" shaped, sunken room extended almost to the cave roof. The walls were six or seven feet high and perfectly preserved. The top of the cave served as a roof for the structure. On the left side of the ruin, a stairway of stone slabs descended into the sunken room. A rock-lined fire pit was centered on the floor. The roof of the cave was soot-stained and dirty.

Outside of the ruin, but still in the shelter of the overhang, a large square rock, about the size of a desk, held Anasazi fingerprints hardened in clay where mud for the walls or clay pots had been mixed like bread dough. In front of the rock shelter and down the slope below it, the ground was littered with beautiful pottery fragments and splinters of flint chips.

I was so excited. I had seen several Anasazi ruins, but someone had always shown them to me. This was the first one I had ever discovered on my own. This one was mine. Reed and I climbed all over the place. We were on a treasure hunt. We were excited, exploring, and sorting through pottery fragments. We peeked into cracks and crevices in the rocks and followed the trail of flint chips down the slope in front of the ruin.

I found a piece of ancient cotton string about six inches long, and a fragment of an atlatl dart. The dart shaft was a stout river reed with a polished hardwood fore shaft embedded in one end and secured with animal sinew. It looked like it had been deliberately broken. The cane shaft was snapped off and the hardwood dart shaft broken just above where the dart point should have been. I was very disappointed when I couldn't find the rest of it. The artifacts were perfectly preserved. The dry cave had done a marvelous job of protecting the fragile remains. We found some large chunks of dried squash rind, some corncobs and some strange plant fragments that Grandpa thought were cotton bolls.

We ran back to Grandpa and showed him our loot. He was instantly incredulous. He just couldn't believe there was actually a big ruin very near where he had spent so much time and he didn't know about it. He was interested now, and he walked all the way back with us to check it out.

Grandpa was amazed. He walked through the ruin and he kept saying over and over, "I'll be damned … I'll be damned." I was proud as punch, and thrilled to give him a guided tour of "my" Moki castle.

We didn't disturb the ruin. We didn't dig any holes or write our names or litter. We treated her with dignity and respect. We did look hard for artifacts, but the few items described were the only things we found and they were sticking up out of the dirt of the cave floor.

Sadly, today my Moki castle is somewhere at the bottom of Lake Powell. I am honored that the winds of fate allowed me to embrace her before the cold water found her, but my heart bleeds that I cannot show her to my Grandchildren. We didn't have a camera on that trip, and I didn't make it back before she was gone.

Just a few years earlier, in 1954 or '55, Uncle Jack had a man named Dave Rich working for him in Red Canyon on the Smith Company uranium claims. Mr. Rich's young daughter Anice found a perfect Anasazi clay pot in a small cave near the river. We already knew the story, the Rich family lived in Wellington and we played with the Rich kids all the time. Grandpa pointed out the area where Anise had found the pot, and brother Reed and I went exploring and found the place.

Back inside the cave, we could still see where the clay pot had been dug out of dried mud that had seeped in from centuries of rainwater. There was still a cast of the pot like a clay mold in the wall of the cave. There were also rotted basketry fragments there. The clay pot had been sitting in a woven basket. I tried to rescue some of the basket but it fell apart in my fingers. It was as fragile as a spider's web. The damp mud had ruined it.

That corrugated clay pot is one of a precious few to be rescued from the cold waters of Lake Powell. Hundreds, if not many thousands of others, were not. Dr. Jesse Jennings and students from the University of Utah swept through the canyons just ahead of the lake waters doing archaeological salvage work. They found some of the more obvious and easy-to-salvage sites, but they know, and I know, that most of what was there was never found or rescued.

A trip to Red Canyon

The clay pot Anice Rich Behunin found in Red Canyon can still be seen today. It sits proudly in the Museum of the San Rafael in Castle Dale, Utah, about thirty miles south of Price. The museum of the San Rafael is one of Utah's best-kept secrets, and well worth the effort to stop and see.

We spent that day and the morning of the following day, at the uranium claims. Reed and I walked along a low gravel bar near the river and threw sticks and stones into the current. We could look far down the river into the shadowy depths of Glen Canyon.

The river was different there than in White Canyon. In White Canyon the river flowed through a valley of rich, red dirt that extended right down to the riverbank. In Red Canyon, the riverbank was gravel mixed with big rocks and boulders. Red Canyon was different from White Canyon in other ways too. The feel of the place was different. It was lonesome, cold and empty. The sun hid behind an overcast sky and even the big river hurried past, eager to be gone. The river went innocently on her way, unaware that the canyon below would soon be filling up with cement and she might be delayed by construction.

Many years later, in the mid-1980s, I started into Red Canyon again. It was my intent to go as far as I could to see where the water had backed up and what was left of the place. My sweet wife Jeannie and I started down that long and narrow dirt road, and it hadn't changed much since the 1950s. We traveled several miles on the backside of Mars.

And, as we descended into the depths of the canyon, I began to feel again that same uneasiness I had felt so many years before while camping with Grandpa near the Red House Cliffs. The feeling was even stronger this time, and it came upon me in the full light of day. It was a feeling of utter vulnerability, with a foreboding chill. I felt creepy and uneasy. I stopped the truck and told Jeannie all about it.

We didn't go all the way to the lake. I just couldn't do it. From where we turned around we could see the flat water of the lake shining in the distance. But we didn't go there. I can't explain my uneasy feelings about the place, but as soon as we breached the Red House Cliffs and could see Cedar Mesa and the Bears Ears again, I was free. The dark, foreboding gloom melted away. The desert is a place of mystery, and for some reason, Red Canyon doesn't like me much. The feeling is mutual.

On our way home with Grandpa on that 1950s trip, it snowed on us. It started raining near Natural Bridges and the Bears Ears were wet and cold as we made our way across. Snow started falling heavily as we approached Blanding and Grandpa said he was glad we had made it over Elk Ridge before the snow got deep. That little two-wheel-drive pickup truck was a keeper, but we would have had to use tire chains if we had stayed an hour longer. It snowed and rained on us all the way home to Wellington. We got home late that night in the dark and the storm.

I don't know if Grandpa ever went back to Red Canyon after that. If he did, he didn't take us boys.

17
Nineteen Fifty Nine

My last trip to White Canyon with Grandpa was in December, 1959. It was just a few days after my thirteenth birthday. Grandpa was going to the desert again to do assessment work on his uranium claims. He asked if Reed and I would like to go along. We were thrilled. I hadn't been there for a while and I knew the canyon would soon be underwater. I had been given a little box camera for my birthday, and I was excited by the opportunity to take some pictures before Lake Powell covered my favorite place forever.

Before we even started, I had a feeling about that trip, a premonition I suppose. Somehow I knew this would be my last visit to that special place of my childhood. I was going to White Canyon to say goodbye.

It was wintertime and the weather was cold. I remember that trip vividly. I was very much aware that we were going to a special place I might never see again. I desperately chiseled every image into my memory like landscapes in granite. I Looked long and hard at everything, determined to remember and preserve, if only in my mind, the sights, sounds and feel of that special place.

With my little camera, I had been given a couple of rolls of black and white film. I had one roll left when Grandpa called. It was a roll of twelve exposures. That single roll of black and white film was my only chance to capture the image and the essence of Glen Canyon before Lake Powell swallowed it up. I knew it was a daunting task, and I wished I had better equipment and a bucket full of film, but I had to make do with what I had. I spent each frame as dearly as I knew how. I took pictures only of things I considered to be important, irreplaceable, and soon to be lost. Five of the pictures in this little book were taken from that roll of film.

There was little traffic in those days between Wellington and Green River on Highway 6. It was a good paved road, but narrow and winding by today's standards. We were approaching the old ghost town of Woodside as the sun was coming up, and we had the road all to ourselves. We were purring along with the sun in our eyes when suddenly an animal appeared in the road some distance in front of us. The animal stood frozen for a moment, its outline blurred by the morning haze. We thought at first it was a large dog, but then, as we got closer, it turned away and began a slow, leisurely lope toward the Book Cliffs. A long tail floated gracefully in its wake like the tail on a kite.

"By damn – that's a mountain lion!" Grandpa said with a gasp of disbelief. He slammed the Chevy to a stop in the gravel on the shoulder of the road, jumped out and fished under his seat. He came up with a black leather gun belt all rolled together and he fumbled with excitement as he dug the revolver out. The big cat was loping away across the sand flats, opening and closing like a pair of scissors as he crossed the open country. His yellow-gray coat sheened in the morning light and his muscles rippled with each leisurely bound. He was moving fast, but his movements were so fluid and graceful it looked like he was putting little effort into his escape.

The revolver barked at the big cat: pop-pop-pop-pop. Grandpa was shooting fast and holding high to help the bullets reach. Pop-pop-pop-pop-pop, nine shots in all, a full load for the little .22 handgun. The big cat didn't seem to notice. He never looked back, never lost his composure, and never broke stride as little geysers of dirt splashed around him. We watched him disappear into the rough country at the foot of the Book Cliffs, unhurt, unruffled, and still running wild and free.

Grandpa stood for a while with the smoking gun in his hand as he watched the cat fade away. Then he turned to Reed and me with shining eyes and a wide smile and said, "Wasn't that the prettiest thing you ever saw? Damn … could you kids see his muscles? I've never seen anything like that. I sure wish I had my rifle. I could've got him with my rifle."

Grandpa reloaded the pistol and stowed it back under the truck seat, then we started again toward Green River. For the next several miles Grandpa talked excitedly and told us all about mountain lions. And for the next two or three days he mourned that his deer rifle was at home, in the gun rack, on his bedroom wall.

We stopped in Hanksville later that same morning. Grandpa stopped to talk to someone. It might have been Reo Hunt. I'm not sure after all these years. The man knew a lot about rocks and geology, and he and Grandpa showed each other rock specimens and talked and traded prospecting stories. I was bored and anxious to be on our way, but Grandpa would not be hurried. He bought Reed and me each a bottle of pop at the Hanksville store and we threw sticks for the man's dog while he and grandpa talked and smoked and dreamed of finding the mother lode like Charlie Steen.

Finally, we put Hanksville behind us and journeyed into North Wash toward Hite. We camped for the night at Hog Spring, of course, and we camped in the mid-afternoon. It was December and the days were short.

Before we made camp for the night, Grandpa took us on a little hike and showed us what he believed to be some old Spanish writing carved into the rocks. He had found the place some years before when exploring for uranium in the canyon. The site is a large circle scratched into the sandstone with a cross through the middle of it. It is not a Christian cross, but a cross that divides the circle into four equal parts. Below the circle is an inscription that appears to be Latin. The inscription reads, "Anno Kosmon 103." It is a faded rendering, hard to photograph, but it can still be read clearly.

For years my Grandfather kept the location of the site a secret. Surely it was evidence of unknown and forgotten explorers, Spanish Conquistadors undoubtedly, who had journeyed through North Wash in that time when America was still being discovered and gold might be found anywhere.

The inscription was a delicious mystery. For years Grandpa tried to untangle the meaning of the message. He knew Anno meant "year of" as in Anno Domini. But the word Kosmon could not be found in any Latin or Spanish dictionaries. And, who could guess what 103 might mean? Was it a date, a measure of distance, the number of men in the exploring party, or the number of gold bars buried nearby? Who could know for sure?

In the first edition of this book, the author told of the inscription and the mystery surrounding it. He then offered a challenge to anyone who might be able to decipher the inscription and solve the mystery. Just Four years later, in April 2007, an answer arrived when a friend, noted author and historian, James H. Knipmeyer, sent the following email:

> Tom, I was in Salt Lake City doing research at the Utah State Historical Society reading through an interview given by Pearl Baker some years ago. In it she mentioned an incident, sometime in the 1950s, of driving from White Canyon to Blanding and picking up a hitchhiker on his way to the Essenes Kosmon commune in Montrose, Colorado. Of course, the mention of the word "Kosmon" caught my attention. Here is what I have found.

> In 1881 a New York dentist and doctor, John B. Newbrough, claimed that while under "spirit control" he wrote a new bible called Oahaspe. In it was described Kosmon, or the Kosmon Era, a sort of "new world order" where all of the world's people would live harmoniously as one. One of the books of this new bible was the Book of Shalam, which set forth a plan for gathering the outcast and

orphaned children of the world and raising them, according to strict religious principles, to be the spiritual leaders of this new Kosmon age.

Newbrough and some 20 of his fellow "faithists" decided to create such a place, and in 1884 Shalam Colony was established on the banks of the Rio Grande River, about 6 miles from Las Cruces, New Mexico. Financed by a wealthy wool merchant from Boston, the colony developed into a "showcase" agricultural area. Newbrough died in 1891, and by the end of the decade, for a variety of reasons, the colony fell into decline. In 1901 the remaining children were sent to orphanages and Shalam Colony closed.

However, the work of the Faithists did not end. A new colony was established near Denver in the early 1900s while some of the colonists from Shalam went to California. It was in Los Angeles that Wing Anderson met the Faithists, and under his direction a community was established in North Salt Lake, Utah, in the 1930s. They called themselves, Essenes of Kosmon. In the 1940s the group moved to Montrose, Colorado, where it eventually closed in the 1950s. Even today, the Essenes of Kosmon remain a legally recognized religion.

In 1885, while still in New Mexico, the Faithists published a book entitled, Kosmon Almanac: The New Calendar based on the Movements of Our Solar Phalanx. According to this "new calendar," the Kosmon Era began in 1848, which would make the "Anno Kosmon 103" inscription in North Wash to mean, "Kosmon Year 103" or 1951. So, the circle pictograph and accompanying inscription were made by one of the Faithists in 1951, and like Pearl Baker's hitchhiker, was probably linked to the Montrose, Colorado commune. It is thus NOT a Spanish inscription at all.

Bummer Dude. Not the story we all wanted to hear, but it's the real deal. Thank you, James Knipmeyer, for taking the time to share your findings. Everyone should buy Jim Knipmeyer's books. He does a great job and his latest endeavor (2016) is, *Cass Hite: The Life of an Old Prospector.* Published by the University of Utah. The book is an excellent biography of that fascinating character who founded the town of Hite and found gold along the Colorado River.

Nineteen Fifty Nine

It was cold camping in North Wash that winter's night back in 1959, but we were well prepared. Grandpa was always tinkering and inventing, and he had rigged up a tent-cover for the back of the truck. That windy night at the top of Red Canyon might have been his inspiration. He made a wooden frame that looked like a set of outdoor clothesline poles that fastened to the truck bed, front and back with metal clamps. A long wooden pole with metal joints bridged the two halves and formed the ridgeline for a tent. Over this frame he stretched the canvas tarp he kept his camp gear wrapped up in. He secured the tarp with tie-downs bolted to the side of the pickup bed. It was an ingenious invention in those days before camper shells. It worked very well and kept the cold night air and morning frost away. The only drawback was, we couldn't watch the stars as we fell asleep.

The next morning we ate breakfast around a smoky cottonwood campfire. Bacon and eggs with warmed-up homemade biscuits and butter. It was cold in the shadows of the canyon. Reed and I shivered and snuggled close to the weak and stinky little campfire as Grandpa drank a whole pot of coffee, one slurp at a time. Grandpa loved his coffee and he lingered over it. He would drink from his tin cup and then chase the hot liquid down with warm tobacco smoke. The sweet incense of tobacco was a joy after the bitter stench of damp cottonwood smoke. Boys didn't drink coffee, or smoke, so we huddled, shivered, waited and wished the coffee pot dry.

Finally, the coffee ran out and we snuffed out the smoky fire, loaded up and continued our journey to the Colorado River and Hite. We broke out of North Wash in the late morning and the river was happy to see us there. I hadn't seen her for a long time, but she recognized me and she welcomed me back. She was weaker and more humble than I remembered. She was growing old. The water was low and had that cold, iron gray color of winter. Long white sandbars lined her channel like beaches along the ocean. The water was flat and calm. No flexing of liquid muscle from the middle of the channel this time.

But then of course, I knew there was still hope. It was wintertime and the river was in hibernation. In the coming spring she would be born anew. The numberless side canyons would feed her a thick, loamy broth from the distant snowfields and the runoff would be seasoned with rich, red soil. The river's cheeks would blush healthy again and she would rise like the phoenix to fill her deep and sandy channel. It had happened every year, for thousands and thousands of years.

The Hite ferry was still as I remembered it. Grandpa stopped at the house to visit with the ferryboat operator and his wife. I don't remember their names, but they were delighted to have company at their lonely duty station. The woman was friendly and put on a fresh pot of coffee. Grandpa pulled up a chair. Reed and I knew he would be there for a while. I excused myself and walked over to where the ferryboat was moored. I took the first of my twelve precious pictures.

While Grandpa drank coffee and visited with the ferryboat people, Reed and I climbed a rocky hill above the ferry site to go exploring. We found some good petroglyph panels. One panel was a row of five handsome warriors with what appeared to be feathers protruding from their heads. The panel was carved on a low rock wall, but hidden behind some large boulders. The warriors were hiding there, out of sight like a war party, waiting to ambush the stagecoach. With some distress, I looked at the big river nearby and knew the dark water would soon find their hiding place. I wanted to save those handsome warriors, so I carefully took another of my twelve pictures.

Hite Ferry, view to the east toward White Canyon.
Author photo, December 1959

Reed and I climbed around in the rocks for an hour or more. We found another rock art panel of warriors with shields, and I couldn't resist. I spent another precious frame. Then, as we got closer to the crest of the hill, we found the signature of old Cass Hite himself. The inscription was fairly large and in an antique cursive style. It was on a discrete rock face and not visible until a person stood right in front of it. It was chiseled into the everlasting stone with a bold hand ... *Cass Hite 1883.*

From the inscription, we could look down on the farm, the ferryboat landing and the entire little corner of wilderness Cass Hite had claimed as his own. I held the little camera in my hands and agonized about taking a picture of the inscription. I only had nine frames left and we weren't even on the White Canyon side of the river yet. I decided to save the film and take pictures of more interesting things later on. Later that morning, as we prepared to cross the river on the ferryboat, I told Grandpa about Cass Hite's name on that rock. He seemed genuinely interested, but it was going to be a long day and we needed to cross the river. He didn't go with us to see it like I hoped he would.

I don't know if the ferryboat people ever saw the inscription, or if anyone ever recorded the site before the water covered it. Today that bold pioneer signature is in the mud at the bottom of the lake, and what I wouldn't give to have that picture now.

We crossed the river on the ferryboat. The water was low and the ferry cables hung high overhead. We left the boat, waved goodbye to the ferry operator, and drove the short distance to the old town site.

I knew the town was gone. I had been there a few times since everyone had moved out. But I was not prepared for what I saw that day. Not only was the town gone, her very foundations had been plowed under.

Only the purple-gray tailings pile remained where the mill, the company buildings and the boarding house had stood. Across the White Canyon wash, the store was gone, and so were all of the other buildings. The ground had been scraped and bladed smooth. The place looked like a parking lot ready for asphalt. Only the schoolhouse remained, alone and empty. It was the gutted shell of a once-happy building, echoing the wind and full of drifting red dirt and the tracks of vermin.

The ground was scarred with old truck and bulldozer tracks, preserved in frozen mud. The refuse and rubble of a once thriving little community had been pushed into piles and burned. Some of what had stood there had been hauled off to places like Blanding and Moab, but most of it had fed the funeral pyres of the little town. There were several big burned spots on the ground where odd pieces of wire and metal reached up from the ashes like the limbs of dead and dying creatures.

I suspect it was people from the Vanadium Corporation who had bulldozed everything and set the rubble on fire. White Canyon had been a company town, and the only building left standing was the school, which had probably been deeded to the State of Utah. After the town died, there had been a lot of old scrap lumber, barrels, trash, and tires scattered about, and the shells of a few tarpaper buildings. I'm guessing that the company was told to clean it up before the waters of the lake made some of it float.

The dirt airfield was still there, but there were no airplanes and the sun-bleached old windsock drooped sadly on its metal pole. The harsh wind had beaten the windsock to a tattered rag, a poor remnant of the bright scarlet flag of yesterday. Weeds and baby sage bushes were sneaking out onto the airfield. Bill Wells and his airplane hadn't been there in a long time.

Even the weather was somber and depressing. The sun hid behind a gray overcast and the air was cold. We were wearing jackets and gloves for the first time I could remember in that usually warm and welcome corner of the desert. The town site was eerily quiet, and for the first time ever in the canyon, I noticed that when we slammed the door of the pickup truck we could hear the echo in the ledges.

Grandma's house was still there, filled with dust, cobwebs and packrat poop. It had been standing alone in the desert for over three years by then. The two buildings were vacant shells, empty of furniture and warmth. Our voices echoed in the bare rooms in the same way the truck door echoed in the ledges. The feel and the love of my Grandmother wasn't there anymore, and without her the place was only a shed on the cold desert floor. The buildings were so depressing to me I didn't take a picture of them, a decision I have since regretted.

We camped in the yard and slept in the back of the pickup truck. Grandpa cooked over a campfire made from radioactive old boards salvaged from the uranium mill. I asked Grandpa why his house was still standing while all the others were torn down and gone. He said if he didn't move them by a certain date, people from the government would come and burn them down. He never moved the houses, and the ashes of Grandma's house were scattered by the rising waters of Lake Powell.

The second day we were there, Grandpa was busy with grownup things that didn't interest young boys. We talked him into taking us back to the old town site so we could look for arrowheads and take some pictures of the old Indian fort. He left us there alone, and told us to walk the mile or two back to Grandma's house when we were ready. It was another dark and gloomy winter day. It was also creepy to be left alone with the ghosts of that pillaged and burned village of my childhood.

We climbed up to the old Indian fort that guarded the river canyon, good old Fort Moki. She watched us climb the hill to her and she was happy to see us again. She didn't get many visits from little boys anymore.

It felt different to be up there by ourselves. It had never been allowed before. When we had been there years before, Grandma had always insisted that we have a guardian, someone to look after us to keep us from falling off the ledge. Now we stood on that airy height alone, two big boys, one barely thirteen, the other almost eleven.

That dark winter day was our final chance to say goodbye to the Garden of Eden. It was quiet there that day. We had the old fort and the river valley all to ourselves. Our voices echoed from inside the ruin and we stood on that crumpled north wall and looked out over the valley for a long time.

The reality of the Glen Canyon Dam hung heavy like a dark cloud on the southern horizon. There was a feeling of sadness in the air. A hurtful knowing that the ruin, the valley, and the river would soon be gone.

Things were very different from what we remembered as little boys. We were looking down on emptiness. The mill was gone, the town was gone, and there were no shadows of cotton ball clouds in the valley. The day was cold and quiet. Even the sun didn't shine.

The ruined fort had a strange feeling of emptiness about it too. It was the same feeling Grandma's house had held, and I was amazed. At other times the ruin had been warm and friendly. The feel of the Anasazi had been very close and personal. Strangely, on that dark winter's day, the old fort was an empty shell, an open stone box on a hill. The Anasazi didn't live there anymore.

Grandpa had told us that the water would be deep enough to cover the fort, but I could scarcely bring myself to believe it. I looked out over that river valley and could not imagine water being that deep. I tried to visualize what the canyon would look like covered with water, but my imagination failed me. My mind rebelled at the thought and refused to form the image.

I had nine frames left in my little box camera and I willingly spent at least four of them on the old Indian fort. I photographed her from different angles, trying to get her good side and preserve a portrait for the ages. She was wonderfully photogenic, but my equipment was crude, the light was bad, and my fingers trembled.

White Canyon

Fort Moki
Author photo - December, 1959

I took another of my photographs while standing on the crumpled north wall of the fort. I aimed my little camera up the valley, over the empty spot where the town had been, toward where a long, thin shaft of sunlight spilled down through the clouds and fell across the red hills near Grandma's empty house.

Nineteen Fifty Nine

View from Fort Moki looking down on abandoned White Canyon town site in 1959. Brush and trees in center is White Canyon Wash. Uranium tailings pile in foreground. The single building (white spot) at right center is the old school house. Grandma's house is up the canyon near the strip of sunshine on the red hills. View is north. The big ledge and the river road from North Wash (unseen) are on the left across the river.
Author photo.

It broke my heart when we finally said goodbye to the old fort and started down the steep hill toward the canyon bottom. I felt like a traitor. I was walking away and leaving her to her fate, just as the Anasazi had done so many years before.

As we descended the rocky slope below the ruin, the ground was covered with fragments of beautiful Anasazi pottery. The ragged shards begged and reached up to me. I went from piece to piece, lifting them reverently from the dirt and wiping away the dust of centuries. Each fragment was a treasure, each treasure a story all by itself. I marveled at the beauty, the symmetry of design and the brilliant hues of the colors after so many years in the dirt. Each fragment was a precious parting gift from the Anasazi, a ceramic teardrop from the very heart of native culture. They were precious pearls to me, and I wanted to save every one.

White Canyon

Like tiny starfish, stranded and doomed on the shores of the sea, I wish I could have saved them all. I filled my pockets and my hat, desperate to rescue as many as I could. But it was an impossible task. There were just too many and I was so small. I tried anyway, knowing it was hopeless, and my heart hurt.

Reed and I finally made our way down from the battlements and bid the old fort goodbye forever. We followed an ancient trial down to the bottom of the canyon, then crossed White Canyon wash to where we knew there were other ruins.

The other ruins were tucked close against a high, south-facing ledge not far from the road. In earlier years, when we were just little kids, we chased lizards and gathered pockets of flint chips and pottery fragments in the sand dunes at the base of the hill. We were big boys now, and for the first time ever we climbed all the way up to where the ruins were. We were curious, and going to a place we had never been allowed to visit before.

A long row of stonewalls lay exposed in the weak sunlight. They had been houses at one time, and they were sectioned into squares and rectangles with only the top foot or so of the walls showing above the sand. I was surprised to see that they had not been dug up. Grandpa told us that people from the university were going to come and excavate all the ruins and salvage all of the artifacts before the water backed up. No one from the university had been to that place yet.

Like the old Moki fort, the talus slope below the ruin was covered with pottery shards and flint chips. We poked around on the hillside for an hour or two searching for artifacts. Reed found two good arrowheads. I wanted so very much to find a souvenir to take home with me that day, but in spite of my best efforts, I found nothing. Brother Reed, knowing my passion for all things Anasazi, graciously gave me his.

I have often thought about that long row of stonewalls and wondered what secrets might have been hiding there. To my knowledge, no one from the university ever investigated that site. Like my Moki Castle in Red Canyon, and Fort Moki across the wash, those stone walls remain today one of the thousands of archaeological treasures lost in the cold waters of the lake.

Reed and I never saw another person in the canyon that day. Everything was quiet, vacant and somber. As we grew tired, cold and hungry, we moved lower and lower down the talus slope until we reached the dirt road at the bottom of the hill. The road would take us back to where Grandpa was.

We had no sooner reached the road than we found lion tracks! Actually, from my far-removed and adult perspective of today, I suspect they were big dog tracks. Probably a mutt belonging to someone from the search and destroy brigades that had knocked the town down and burned it. There was nothing at all in White Canyon for a mountain lion to eat unless he had a thing for lizards. All the deer and other cat cuisine were on the mountain and foothills of Elk Ridge many miles away.

However, in one of those rare and silly twists of irony, we had both seen our very first, wild and dangerous mountain lion on the way to White Canyon just a day or two before. Mountain lions were very real to us now. To make matters worse, Grandpa had told us long and scary stories about mountain lions and how they will stalk any prey and pull down a full-grown horse. Mountain lions had been heavy on our minds and in our dreams the past few days. And to top it all off, Grandpa had told us that lion tracks look just like big dog tracks!

The tracks we found were old and nearly fossilized in the dried mud, but that didn't interfere with our boyish imaginations one little bit. The canyon was empty and eerily quiet all around us. We suddenly felt very vulnerable and desperately all alone. We just knew we were about to become some big lion's lunch, and we took off down that dusty road like Olympic sprinters.

No kids ever covered a mile and a half any faster than we did. And we did most of it jogging backwards with rocks in our hands. From behind every rock and bush I fully expected to see some huge, drooling, red-eyed and yellow-fanged monster stealing up on us. I could just imagine him sailing through the air to take us out in a splash of guts and gore. I could clearly remember the long tail and the rippling muscles of the big cat of yesterday, and I knew we were doomed.

We sprinted the last few hundred yards back to Grandpa. We were gasping and out-of-breath. We excitedly told him about the old devil-cat that had chased us back to the truck. Grandpa listened with a great deal of interest, but a condescending twinkle crept into his eye. I was frustrated because I knew he didn't believe how close we had come to being lion dung out there in the desert. And while I couldn't honestly say that I had actually seen the old devil-cat, I just knew he was there, and that's all there was to it. Our close call with a violent death was very real to Reed and me, and we stayed pretty close to that old man for the rest of that trip.

That afternoon we puttered around Grandma's old place. I wanted to go exploring again, but I just knew the big cat was lurking out there somewhere, ready to rip my guts out and turn me into Spam. Reed and I decided to do our exploring close to camp where it was safer, and where Grandpa could hear our plaintive screams when the lion pounced on us.

We walked up on the little ridge behind Grandma's house where we used to play, keeping one eye on the ledges to be sure the lion didn't get the drop on us. The sun peeked out cautiously from an overcast sky and smiled down on us. We were on old familiar ground. We had played there many times in years past while Grandma hovered near.

It knocked the wind out of me when I found the perfect arrowhead. It was a beautiful Basketmaker dart point, almost two inches long. It was made of dark brown chert and lying right on top of the ground like it had fallen from the sky. I couldn't believe it. At the Indian ruins above town I had almost blown the gaskets in my eyeballs I had tried so hard to find a good arrow point. And now, right behind Grandma's house, I had found a good one without even looking for it.

I held that arrowhead in my trembling hand and studied it for several minutes. I couldn't believe it had been there all of those years. The ground was open and bare. Grandma and Grandpa and all of us kids had been over that ground dozens of times. As kids we had played there and rolled tires all over that spot. We had chased lizards, thrown rocks and eaten picnic lunches there. That pretty arrowhead wasn't there back then.

It was a gift. There was no other explanation. I just knew that one of my unseen Anasazi friends had planted it there for me to find. The Anasazi knew my heart, and they knew I would never be back. They knew there was nothing I could take home as a memento of that river canyon that would mean more to me than that perfect arrowhead. To find it behind Grandma's house was a special bonus.

I kept that arrowhead in my hand, deep inside my jersey glove, for the next day and a half. I kept my fingers safely tucked around it until we were home, and then I wrapped it in cotton and put it in my arrowhead box. I still have it and it is more precious than diamonds to me. That single, perfect arrowhead is my one shining contribution to the archaeological salvage work done in Glen Canyon. I wish I could have done more.

The next morning we started for home. The day was much warmer and we shed our winter jackets. We crossed the river on the ferryboat and stopped to visit with the ferryboat people again. Reed and I were too afraid of lions to go back up on the hill by Cass Hite's signature, and besides, I didn't have any film left in my little camera. The nice ferryboat lady made us kool-Aid while the men drank coffee.

Then, before we left, the ferryboat lady and her husband gave us gift. They stepped into a shed near their house and talked for a moment, and when they came out the man handed us a sled. It wasn't a normal sled. It was a big, super-duper, Flexible Flyer with a custom paint job and honest to goodness soft rubber hand grips to boot. The nice lady said they didn't get much snow at Hite, but maybe we could find some snow where we lived. It took Reed and me, and three other little brothers to finally wear that sled out. Thank you, nice ferryboat lady, wherever you are.

When we finally left Hite for that last time, Grandpa stopped for a while near the mouth of North Wash. He said he wanted to show us something. He pulled the truck off the road and into the tamarack bushes near a flat place by the river. We walked through the tamaracks a short distance to where an old rock chimney towered high above the willows. Around the chimney were scattered a few old planks, rusted barrel hoops, tin cans, broken slivers of purple glass and other odd bits of trash. The junk was sinking into the weeds and dirt. There were a few notched and decaying cottonwood logs strewn about, remnants of the log cabin that had once been wrapped around the chimney. We didn't know it at the time, but the chimney marked the location of "Crescent City," that hardscrabble gold camp frequented by Robert Stanton in the late 1880s.

Grandpa took us toward the river, through the tamaracks, to where a big wooden post was planted firmly in the willows. The post was almost hidden in a thick tangle of bushes and Grandpa had to search for a few minutes to find it. The post was bleached from years in the sun and the uncaring tamaracks had crowded right up against it. When he finally found it, he pointed out where scars and rope burns dug deep into the wood. The heavy post stood just back from the river on a sandy bar that held it slightly elevated above the level of the river floods.

Grandpa stood near the post and pointed at the river.

"This is the Dandy Crossing of the Colorado," he said with an air of absolute conviction.

"People think it was down at the ferry site, but it wasn't."

He then pointed out some features of the river.

"Can you see how the river makes a bend here?" he asked.

"The current changes sides here, twice.

"We are standing in the middle of the bend. The current is right up against the shore here at our feet.

"If you get in the water here, the current will take you across the river to the other side.

"If you are on the other side of the river, all you do is go upstream a little ways and the current is at your feet over there. If you get in the river there, the current brings you here to where we are standing."

It was so obvious.

He continued: "This post was a brace to help pull wagons or rafts up out of the river. There might have been another one on the other side of the river. I looked for it, but couldn't find it.

"The tamarack wasn't here when Cass Hite used this crossing and a horse was used to pull a rope against this cedar brace. That's why the rope cut so deep into the wood."

He continued, "Cass Hite moved down to the ferry site because he could farm down there.

"The current is near the middle of the river down where the Hite ferry is and the river is deep. It would be a dangerous place to cross.

"And another thing," he said, "The east side of the Hite ferry landing is at the foot of a long ledge. It would have been a lousy place to get wagons or a herd of horses out of the river."

He pointed at the river again.

"Right here is where the Indians and the early pioneers crossed the river. This is Cass Hite's Dandy Crossing of the Colorado."

He stood looking at the river for a long time as if watching it all happen. I looked at the river too, and while I stood there, painted Indians on beautiful horses, Spanish Conquistadors, cowboys and covered wagons, all swam the river at my feet.

I'm sure Grandpa didn't know that the stone chimney he showed us that day was the ruins of Crescent City. Grandpa was a great storyteller, and had he known, he would have spun some good yarns about it.

Unfortunately, my Grandfather was wrong about the Dandy Crossing. Again, it was James Knipmeyer who gave me compelling information that the ferry post at the mouth of North Wash was from the Harshberger Ferry of 1906. Cass Hite's Dandy Crossing really was at the mouth of White Canyon.

A man named Benjamin Harshberger was mining copper in White Canyon when he planted that big wooden post as a ferry mooring. For a year or so he tried to haul unprocessed copper ore in wagons to the railroad at Green River. The haulage was way too expensive, and like all of the old miners in Glen Canyon, Mr. Harshberger went broke.

Nineteen Fifty Nine

The old ferry post at the Mouth of North Wash
A remnant of the Harshberber Ferry of 1906

Then, Maurine Dorman recently gave the author another interesting story about the location of Dandy Crossing. In a collection of old files and photos gathered by her late husband, Dr. J. Eldon Dorman, was an unpublished manuscript written by well-known Canyon Country historian, Pearl Baker, in 1988. In the manuscript, Baker tells of asking one of the old-time, part-time residents of Glen Canyon, a man named Frank Barrett, where he thought the Dandy Crossing was. Pearl Baker was teaching school in White Canyon at the time, so the date would have been in the early 1950s.

They were standing on the river bank at the mouth of White Canyon, very near the boardinghouse and the uranium tailings pile from the mill, when Barrett told her, "You are standing on it [Dandy Crossing]. It lies across the fan of rocks and gravel that White Canyon has shot out into the Colorado during floods. The river smoothes out these rocks so that there is no dam, but they pave the crossing all the way. Going from this [east] side over, the crossing aims downstream over this fan, coming out right down there, but you don't go downstream too much. From that side over to this, it comes out below the mouth of the [White] canyon, but there is plenty of room and good banks."

Barrett also told her that many years before he and "another fellow" had wintered at the mouth of White Canyon and by early February they were low on grub. The road over the Bears Ears was closed by snow and the only way to town was across the river and up North Wash. He said they gathered driftwood along the river and made a large raft, using four empty gas barrels for extra buoyancy. They then crossed over Dandy Crossing with their Model T Ford lashed on top of the raft. On the western shore they took Cass Hite's old wagon road up North Wash to Hanksville and Green River, then on to Dove Creek, Colorado and home.

I just can't help but admire men like that. Those early White Canyon dwellers were very brave and resourceful "fellows."

As we turned up North Wash, leaving the Harshberger ferry post and the ruins of Crescent City behind, we boys began pestering Grandpa that we wanted to stop at Hog Spring and say hello to the Moki Queen. It just didn't seem right to drive past that Indian Princess without stopping to pay our proper respects.

When we got to Hog Spring there was a man and a woman camped there, which surprised us. I couldn't remember other people ever camping there. I thought Hog Spring was our secret, private place, and I was annoyed by the intrusion.

The people were strangers and they looked out-of-place on the desert. They were probably in their late twenties or early thirties and they were driving a silly little car out there in the rocks and gravel where everyone who knew better drove a pickup truck. The little car had an ugly gypsy rack on top that was bulging with suitcases, gas cans and camping gear. There was a canvas tarp spread on the ground near the little car, and on it were a thin cotton mattress, several blankets, pillows, and clothes.

The people were dressed like foreigners. He was wearing a fedora type hat, dress pants (slacks) and a silky, short-sleeved shirt. He was also wearing low cut city shoes out there in the sand, and that made me smile. She was decked out in tiger-striped pedal-pusher pants, a short-sleeved blouse with the tails tied in a knot around her middle, and slippers. Her hair was tied up in a red bandana and she looked like Lucille Ball doing a comedy sketch.

We got out of the truck and said hello to them politely and cautiously. I'm sure we were staring way too much at their improbable clothes, transportation and camp outfit. Grandpa made polite small talk for a few minutes before he noticed something unusual and utterly disgusting on the ledge beyond the spring. When he saw it, he stood with his mouth open for a moment. He then pointed and asked, "Did you do that?"

The man was stupid, and he nodded innocently, allowing that yes, he had done that. I followed the direction of Grandpa's finger and the bright yellow paint screamed at me when I saw it. There … on that sacred sandstone wall was a gaudy billboard:

Milo and Vivian
San Francisco California 1959

Grandpa came uncorked. I knew he was a scrapper, but I had never seen him with blood in his eye. He was probably thirty years older than Milo, but he stepped right up to the dim-bulbed San Franciscan and stuck his chin out as if daring the man to take his best shot. I don't remember all he said, but do I remember how he said it, and I thought Grandpa restrained his language admirably. After all, the man's wife was present. Suffice it to say that Milo knew right away that he had made a big mistake.

With dark, steely eyes and very careful and measured words, Grandpa told the man that North Wash was our back yard and he didn't want to see old Milo's name every time he came down that road. He told Milo that he didn't give a damn who he was or where he came from. He asked Milo how he would feel if one of us went to California and painted our name on the side of his DAMNED HOUSE !

Grandpa was fuming and Milo looked like he was going to be sick. But Milo might have been smarter than I knew. He wisely didn't say anything and just stood there stupidly with his mouth open. I thought for a moment that Vivian was going to abandon Milo to his fate and flee into the ledges like a prairie chicken. She stood with both hands over her mouth, eyes wide in panic.

We didn't stay long at the Moki Queen that afternoon. In fact, we didn't even get to visit her. Grandpa was upset and anxious to be gone. We were soon headed for Hanksville. Grandpa held the steering wheel in both hands and puffed on his cigarette like Popeye the Sailorman. He said it was a good thing we didn't show Milo and Vivian where the Moki Queen was, the sorry (expletives deleted) would have probably painted over it.

As we left, Milo and Vivian were breaking camp and hurrying to get out of there before Grandpa changed his mind and came back to visit with them again. Vivian was dumping armloads of camp gear into the back of the little car like she was taking out the trash. Milo was on his knees, rolling up the bedding while pretending that he still had the strength to walk, if he really wanted to.

They were the first real tourists I ever encountered on my red desert. Sadly, they were the spearhead of an invasion.

18
Reflections

I didn't go back to see White Canyon until the summer of 1980. It had been more than twenty years since that last trip with Grandpa, and ironically, it was the year that Lake Powell crested. The wet claws of the lake were reaching three miles up White Canyon Wash, and farther south, Rainbow Bridge was standing in water up to her ankles. The dead water was more than 200 feet deep over Grandma's house.

It was hard for me to go back. For years I had resisted it. It was like returning to the place where a loved one had died. I had a heart filled with warm memories and I didn't want to burst that bubble.

But I had to go back. I loved White Canyon and she had been calling me. Her Siren's song, and questions posed by my own little boys, finally compelled me to make the journey. Jeannie and I loaded up our four boys, a little blue dog named Elvis and our camping gear. We went there for summer vacation.

I was eager, yet anxious as we began our journey south. It was like traveling to a family reunion with loved ones not seen in decades. Would the canyon remember me now that I was a grown man? And, what would I think of her now that she had changed so dramatically?

Over the years I had journeyed to Hanksville, Temple Mountain, the San Rafael Swell and the Henry Mountains many times, and so I knew a little of what to expect. I had traveled some of the new paved highways on the desert and I had seen the Smokey-Bear-hat rangers around Goblin Valley. I had also watched long caravans of boat trailers disappear toward the south. But in spite of all that, I also knew I could never go home again.

I was delighted to find that North Wash was still my friend. She was beautiful and just the way I remembered her. The paved highway was something new, and Hog Spring was not a secret camping spot anymore, but I was happy to find no trace of Milo and Vivian. The yellow paint abomination was gone. Someone had scrubbed the sandstone clean.

I took my family to see the Moki Queen and she smiled when she saw me coming up the trail. She stood as tall and as proud as ever. I felt compelled to take my hat off in her presence. We followed a beaten trail of sandal and tennis shoe tracks to her throne room, and a small BLM sign soiled the sand at her feet. But she still stood tall, undefiled, and strong. She was still the very heart and the soul of the canyon and my heart soared with the eagles when I saw her again. We embraced, heart to heart, across that open space of five thousand years.

The Moki Queen - Author photo

At the mouth of North Wash we stopped at the Hite overlook. We walked out on the rim and looked down on that river canyon of my childhood. It was a beautiful day and cotton ball clouds were dragging shadows across the valley.

I couldn't talk for a while. My heart was in my throat. The bright, flat water stretched from ledge to ledge across the river canyon. I was seeing the vision my mind had refused to form back in 1959. I had prepared myself for weeks, but it was still a shock.

That special corner of Southern Utah has changed a great deal in my lifetime. There is pavement there now, and spandex. Grandpa wouldn't know the place. For years I brooded and refused to go there, preferring to live with my memories and the ghosts of the past. But since then, I've reconciled myself to the changes. I've decided that I still love the place, and now I go there as often as I can. The desert sun warms my old bones, the red rocks recharge my batteries, and the night sky still reaches out to touch my heart on those brilliant, moonlit nights. White Canyon does look different today, but she is still the Red Rock Garden of Eden.

It was the Moki Queen who helped me make the transition. On that summer's day in 1980, as I stood before her royal image of things past, she whispered to me not to be sad. She told me that change is a constant and there is nothing you or I can do about it. The people, the desert, the river, and even the canyons themselves, are always changing, for that is what it is to be alive. Things that never change are dead. The canyon country is, and always has been, alive.

She reminded me that the ancient artist who painted her image on that sandstone wall would not have recognized the Anasazi, as the Anasazi would not have recognized Father Escalante. Escalante would not have known Cass Hite, and just a few short years ago, my grandfather would have physically attacked a man wearing spandex shorts, a ponytail and earrings on his red desert. Things change.

I don't own White Canyon anymore like I did when I was a kid. It belongs to everyone now and I'm just a tourist like everyone else. My tribe, like the Anasazi, was compelled to leave the desert many years ago.

The people who live and work there today are mostly transplants without roots in the red sand. They are lovers of the desert, but with minds and memories deep in the cities. Most are government functionaries, or employees of concessionaires.

The Red Rock Garden of Eden has become an aquatic theme park in recent years. Tourists, boaters, fishermen, party animals and sun worshiping Adonis and Aphrodite types claim the blue water and lakeshore coves. At the same time, out on the mesa tops and in the deep canyons, backpackers, mountain bikers, gypsies and old hippies rule a desert that was recently the exclusive domain of cowboys and prospectors.

It does make me sad, yet makes me smile, when I hear some new-age adventurist with a backpack and a sunburned nose talk about the desert like it belongs to only him. I'm a guy who knows better. It really did belong to me and my grandpa once. And now, like the Anasazi, I know that no one ever really owns the place. There is a time and a season for everything. This too will pass.

But in spite of all the changes, I refuse to be unhappy about it anymore. The Moki Queen smiled that day in 1980 as she reminded me that almost everything I knew and loved about White Canyon and the desert as a boy is still there: the spectacular vistas, the canyons, red sand, warm sun, towering rock formations, cotton ball clouds, clean ocean blue sky, and even those stupid blue-bellied lizards.

She whispered that only a fool allows the ghosts of yesterday to hide the angels of today.

19
Epilogue

By the end of 2004 the water level in Lake Powell had dropped more than a hundred feet. Seven years of drought had greatly reduced water flow into the lake. At the same time, an ever-increasing demand for irrigation and municipal water was sucking the lake dry. Utah, Arizona, California and Nevada all had straws in the water. Competition over who could get the most was intense.

And, the lake was disfigured by the receding water. An ugly bathtub ring outlined the full circumference of the lake. Beginning at the water level and reaching 100-feet high into the ledges, the red sandstone was bleached a sickly off-white color as the receding water sucked pigment from the ledges. It was an embarrassing thing to witness. Most lake enthusiasts had never dreamed that fluctuating water levels would leave such an unsightly scar.

There was economic damage too. The water was so low people couldn't launch boats from the Hite Marina anymore and the place had become only a convenience store and gas station. Below the river bridges and at the mouth of the Dirty Devil River, the bare lake bottom had become a trashy and repulsive mud flat. Concrete boat ramps at the Hite Marina ended in the willows far short of the water. Weeds and hardy tamarack sprouts were taking root all along the receding shoreline.

But, for some of us, the fading fortunes of the lake were not all dark and gloomy. The dramatic drop in water level presented a possibility that intrigued me. If the water was that low, what had happened to the old Indian fort at the mouth of White Canyon? Was it possible that Old Fort Moki would be coming out of the water again?

White Canyon

The Hite Marina - Summer 2004
Left to right: the first arrow points to the buildings of the marina. The second arrow points to the concrete boat ramp. The third arrow points to the last houseboats able to use the Hite marina. This photo was taken from the Hite Overlook just south of Highway 95.
Author photo

In November of that year (2004), Jeannie and I, along with Leslie Nielson, a family friend, and Ranger Brett Timm from the National Park Service, hiked out on a rim between White Canyon and Farley Canyon and had a look.

I was so excited when I saw that old Indian ruin exposed to the sunshine. She was barely out of the water, but she had risen from the dead. That old fort was only a pile of rocks now, the ruin of a ruin, but I still recognized her. The high rocky promontory she once sat on was now a narrow causeway out into the lake for a hundred yards or more. Water lapped at the fort's foundations, and she looked humbled, wet and beaten, but she was there where I could see her for the first time in forty years. It was a spiritual experience for me.

But while we could see the ruin, there was a great expanse of deep water between her and where we were standing. She was half-a-mile away, and without a boat, we couldn't get to her. We took a lot of long-range pictures and had a little celebration anyway. We saw no other people at the lake that cold winter's day and there were no boats on the flat blue water.

Epilogue

As we looked at the resurrected ruin through binoculars, it occurred to me that it was possible that no one had been to the old fort yet. There were probably less than a dozen people in the whole world who knew, or cared, that she might have risen from her watery grave. So Jeannie and I began to plot how we might be the first to witness close-up what had happened to her in the past 40-years underwater. It posed a problem for people like us who didn't own a boat.

Resurrected Fort Moki as seen from the north rim of White Canyon in November, 2004. The walls of the ruin are the little dots sticking out of the water near the white arrow. This picture was taken while the water level was still receding. Note the 100-foot-high "bathtub ring" on the distant ledges and the chaff of driftwood scraps on the rocks along the bottom of the picture. Author photo

I studied some maps and found a possible way to get to the old fort overland. It would be a rough route, a hike of many miles while traversing raw, unexplored ground. But what the heck. On my 125,000-scale map, the distance was only an inch or two. I talked Jeannie into it. We were 58 and 57 years old at the time, but in pretty good physical shape, and besides, we hadn't had a real adventure for a long time.

White Canyon

In the early morning of January 30, 2005, we parked our pickup truck at the end of the road in White Canyon Wash and struck out toward the lake. It was cold on the desert, and our plan was to hike down White Canyon as far as possible before scaling the canyon walls on the south side of the canyon. With any luck, we might be able to get within a mile or two or our destination before scaling the canyon wall. But, we soon found ourselves wallowing in mud. Recent rains and retreating lake water had fouled the bottom of the wash with a thick, greasy slime. We had to leave the canyon bottom much sooner than expected and climb to the top of the canyon rim.

It was warmer up on the rim in the weak morning sunshine. But from where we topped-out we could see that going over the top of the canyon like that was going to be a much further trek than we had expected. It was obvious we couldn't cover that many miles and be back to the truck before dark. What to do? We rested and ate a granola bar as we considered our options. Then, Jeannie, bless her heart, said she knew what that old fort meant to me, and she said I might be hard to live with if I didn't get to see it after coming this far and getting this close. So, in spite of the miles and the perils of striking out into the rim rocks on our own, she bravely suggested that we should press on.

We knew what we were risking by going forward. It was January and cold on the desert. We had left many of the things we normally carried in our backpacks back at the truck to save weight. Expecting to be back to the truck before dark, we were carrying only the bare necessities and only a little water.

But, just in case we ran into problems, we had chosen this particular winter's day because of the promise of a full moon. I told her it would be okay to hike in the dark. I remembered nights in White Canyon when I was a boy that were so bright my grandfather could read his newspaper by the light of the moon. With that hopeful expectation, and my amazing powers of persuasion (wink), we stepped out smartly and began covering the miles. We soon discovered an old washed-out scar of a uranium prospector's road from the 1950s that took us almost all the way to our destination.

We reached the old Moki fort in the late afternoon and I was sad to see what had become of that magic stone castle of my childhood. Her twelve-foot walls had collapsed inward. She was now a pile of rocks with only three or four feet of her foundation walls still intact. Her toppled stones only a foot or two above the cold, flat water of the lake. That ancient temple on a hill was crumpled, broken and scattered now, but there was still a quiet dignity about her that made me feel humble and small.

Epilogue

The sky was winter gray, cold and empty. Very much like the last time I had been there, 46-years earlier, in December, 1959. And like 1959, the canyon was perfectly quiet. The stillness was all-consuming, hauntingly lonely and very personal in the vastness of the Glen Canyon Wilderness.

And yet my heart rejoiced. I had never expected to see the old fort again. And now, there she was. She had changed a great deal, but the essence of her power, majesty and mystery still lingered. Her mound of collapsed walls resting triumphantly above the flat water, presiding once more over Glen Canyon.

The author at the ruins of Fort Moki, January 30, 2005
Note his tracks in the still-wet mud

There were no tracks in the mud anywhere around the ruin, and with delight I recognized that we had accomplished something very dear to me. Jeannie and I were undoubtedly the first people to witness the fort's remarkable resurrection. A fitting thing to happen, I thought. All those years before, on the eve of her destruction, I had caressed her walls and bid her a soulful goodbye. And now I was the first to touch her again as she shed the mud and water of decades beneath the waves. I don't think anyone ever felt a closer connection to that old Indian ruin than me. It was an honor to be the first to welcome her home. Jeannie and I spent an hour or more in quiet conversation and deep contemplation in the stillness of the canyon.

Then, as the sun was sinking low in the western sky, we decided we had better give some attention to our current situation. It would be dark soon, and cold. Jeannie is much smarter than I, and she suggested we stay overnight near the fort. There were large boulders nearby where we could take shelter from the wind, and the receding lake had deposited driftwood all around the site. Keeping a fire overnight would be easy.

But, true to my nature, I had made a schedule and I was determined to keep it. We had told our sons we would be home about midnight. We had no cell service there at the lake and no way to tell them of our change of plans. Besides, I had important things to do the next day and I was determined to do them.

We had traveled a long way since sunup, but we were still feeling strong and healthy. Then too, we didn't have sleeping bags or blankets, and spending a night in the dirt around a campfire didn't sound very inviting. So, I reminded my dear wife that tonight Mother Nature had promised to light our way home with one of those glorious full moons White Canyon is famous for. We struck out on our back trail, headed back to the truck.

The light was fading fast when we first heard thunder booming over the desert to the north of us, and we noticed, for the first time, the dark cloudbank beginning to cover the red sky of sunset. We hurried along, expecting that promised full moon to come up and light our way. But the moon didn't show. With rising panic, I realized that the moon too, was being obscured by clouds. Distant lightening flashed and thunder growled.

We were in big trouble. We were caught out on the open mesa with night closing-in all around us, fully exposed to the elements with no shelter and no flashlight. I have never felt so stupid. We had deposited our flashlights in a bag in the truck that morning in an effort to save weight. It could have been a fatal mistake.

As the last of the daylight disappeared, we left the trail and dropped down into a little cove at the side of the trail. We were better protected from lightening there, and from the cold wind. But we were done. Even fools like me know better than to try to negotiate canyon rims in the dark. We sat in the sand with our backs to the wind, hoping the storm would soon be gone. Between us we had one aluminum survival blanket and we shook it out and draped it over our shoulders and backs as we huddled together. But soon we were shivering. Jeannie suggested we cut the blanket in two. We each took half, removed our coats and wrapped our upper bodies with the aluminum foil before replacing our jackets. It was a brilliant idea and we were much warmer that way. But even then, after sitting on the damp ground in the cold wind for only a short while, we were both shivering again and we knew we might be hypothermic before daylight. And, if the storm caught us and we got wet, this cold January night might be our last. The wind was howling and the temperature dropping fast.

We had to do something. I told Jeannie I was going to start a fire, a foolishly hopeful sentiment it seemed, there on that rocky mesa without any trees. The very thought of all that driftwood back at the lake made me want to cuss. What a fool I had been. But we couldn't go back there now. It was as dangerous to go back as it was to go forward. Better to chance freezing than walking off a ledge in the dark.

Using the light of distant lightning flashes to guide me, I walked a few yards down our little cove and began kicking up sage bushes, tumble weeds and Brigham Tea bushes. Luckily, I was wearing a good pair of boots and roots embedded in dry sand gave up easily. I soon returned to my sweet wife with a big armload of stickery fuel for a fire. Jeannie, being a woman raised around horses and the great outdoors, had dutifully prepared a fire pit while I was chasing sage brush down the draw. She had scooped out a depression in the sand to better control a fire and help keep the wind from scattering the ashes. We crumpled up tumbleweed and dry sage twigs and soon had a fire.

But sage is lousy fuel for a fire. It burns hot, but it's like burning cardboard. A sage fire must be tended constantly and it takes a whole lot of sage brush to keep a fire going all night. I must have kicked up half-an-acre of sage and Brigham Tea that night, and my exertions probably kept me as warm as the fire did. Jeannie, for her part, did something remarkable. She gathered a few flat rocks and began putting them in the hot coals. When they were hot, she would scrape them out of the fire and bury them in the sand where we were sitting. Take it from someone who knows. When you are caught out in the elements on a cold winter's night, there is nothing better than a warm sandy place to sit.

The far-off flashes of lightening and the whistling of the wind were worrisome, but after we said our evening prayers, the distant storm subsided. God was good to us, as always. It was still a cold, dark night, but we were finally able to relax. We even laughed and joked a little. I reminded Jeannie we didn't have cell phone service, and since we couldn't tell the boys we were okay, they might have the sheriff's posse out looking for us by morning.

White Canyon

She said we had a more serious problem than that. Without cell service we couldn't order pizza. What a woman. And, she is kind. Not once did she remind me about all of that lovely driftwood and those big sheltering rocks we had walked away from back at the lake. She never said "I told you so" or called me stupid, or anything of the sort, even though I deserved it. Every man should have such a woman.

An aerial view of the confluence of White Canyon (top) and Farley Canyon (bottom) with Lake Powell (at right) taken late fall or early winter 2004 looking south down Glen Canyon. White Canyon town was near the tip of the black arrow, still 100-feet below the water. Fort Moki is on a narrow promontory just a little to the right and below the tip of the white arrow. The line of the white arrow follows roughly the path the author and his wife Jeannie took on January 30, 2005 to hike in to the old fort. The lighter sandstone just above the water is the bathtub ring where the water has receded. The blue arrow is near the place where they had to spend the night. In the top center of the picture, Lake Powell can be seen following Glen Canyon further south past Red Canyon and Ticaboo.
Photo courtesy of Brett Timm

The sun came up big, warm and glorious the next morning. From where we were, we could see that had we continued on down the mesa in the dark,

182

we might very well have stepped off the rim and died that night. We had done the right thing by staying put and making do.

Jeannie had trouble walking that morning. She had foolishly worn a new pair of hiking boots the day before and overnight her feet had swollen. Her toes were badly blistered. I felt terrible because I hadn't realized the extent of her discomfort or her injuries. Once we had committed to go the whole distance, she had been quiet, brave and resigned to her misery, only stopping a couple of times to "rearrange her socks," she said.

She limped the first miles that morning, and walked that last mile to the truck in her stocking feet, carrying her boots in her hands. We had a good first-aid kit in the truck and she was able to clean and dress her wounds. She healed completely in only a few days. We got back to our truck about ten that morning and drove home quickly to tell our sons we were okay. We were happy they hadn't called search and rescue.

We were able to go back in April of that same year (2005) in boats. My aunt and uncle, Jack and Melba Winn, cousin Janis Winn York, her husband Rick and other members of her family, and Leslie Nielson and members of her family, were with us. We had a good reunion and spent a few hours reminiscing about White Canyon Town, Glen Canyon and the Hite Ferry. It was a beautiful day and cotton ball clouds were dragging shadows over the flat blue water of the lake.

We had been there about an hour when our daydreams and family remembrances were interrupted by the intrusion of a noisy little motor boat. The boat came ashore and two young men got out and started up the mud bank to where the old fort waited. One of those young men had a copy of my White Canyon book in his hand and was using the crude, hand-drawn map to orient himself with his surroundings. One of the young men in our party walked over to him and said, "The guy who wrote that book is sitting on that rock over there." They both came over and introduced themselves. They were Chris Peterson, President of the Glen Canyon Institute, and Daniel Glick, a reporter for National Geographic. Mr. Peterson was escorting Mr. Glick to help him do a story about the low water levels of the lake and the things the low water was revealing.

Of course they were interested in interviewing our group for the National Geographic story. We all laughed that it must have been fate that put us all together there that morning. What were the chances? In the shadow of the ruins of old Fort Moki, they were able to interview three generations of people who knew and loved Glen Canyon, all in one setting. It was a remarkable experience.

Resurrected Fort Moki - The Ruins of a Ruin.
Author photo, April 2005

Then, something amazing happened. While being asked about my experiences with Fort Moki, I mentioned that before the lake, the flat sandstone shelf the old fort was sitting on had several pioneer inscriptions carved into the stone like names chiseled into a sidewalk. Mr. Peterson asked where. I pointed at a spot and said, "Over there."

The man went back to his boat and returned with a wooden boat oar. He began, ever so carefully, scraping away the three or four inches of dry mud and silt like he was using a snow shovel. And there they were! Names and dates from the 1800s, perfectly preserved like they had never been under the water. The man with the boat paddle howled with delight and the National Geographic reporter smiled, shook his head and muttered, "I don't believe this. I don't believe any of this."

Jeannie and I haven't been back to see the old fort since that amazing day in April, 2005. Fort Moki belongs to everyone now. But I am so proud my precious Jeannie and I were brave enough, tough enough, and foolish enough, to attempt that overland expedition in the dead of winter to be the first to touch her resurrected walls. We hope the National Park Service will forgive us for burning that half acre of sage brush. It was surely a cheaper option than sending a search and rescue team to recover our frozen bodies.

We do hope all who visit Lake Powell and the ruins of Fort Moki will appreciate our love for the place and treat the ruins, the lake and the canyons with respect. White Canyon is still God's red rock Garden of Eden. And it will remain so, long after you and I are gone.

Notes:

1. The full story of the author and his wife Jeannie hiking in to visit the ruins in January 2005 was published in Blue Mountain Shadows Magazine under the title, *Overland to Fort Moki*, in the magazine's 20th anniversary issue, Volume 34/Spring 2006.

2. The National Geographic article was published in the April 2006 issue under the title, *A Dry Red Season: Drought drains Lake Powell - uncovering the glory of Glen Canyon.*

Tom McCourt

435-637-4544
southpaw@emerytelcom.net

Southpaw Publications

Epilogue

Other works by the Author:

The Split Sky: A Journey of Discovery in Utah's Nine Mile Canyon
A delightfully humorous tale of the author's adventures as a 16-year-old wanna-be cowboy while working for Utah's largest privately owned cattle ranch in 1963.

To Be A Soldier
A memoir of coming of age in the 1960s, being drafted and serving in the Vietnam War. A personal story of service, sacrifice and the moral and social turmoil of the 1960s. This book has been used as a text by two Utah high schools. No bad language.

The Moab Story: Cowpokes to Bike Spokes
A brief and entertaining outline of the history of Moab, Utah, told through short stories.

Last of the Robber's Roost Outlaws: Moab's Bill Tibbetts
The true story of a 1920s cowboy who broke jail in Moab and hid out in the Robber's Roost on horseback, where the sheriff could never catch him. A colorful and intriguing tale that contrasts what Bill Tibbetts told his family and what the sheriff was telling the newspapers. A great story that documents the end of the Old West in Southeast Utah.

King of the Colorado: The Story of Cass Hite, Utah's Legendary Explorer, Prospector and Pioneer
A historical novel about the man who lived among the Navajos, founded the town of Hite, discovered Utah's Natural Bridges National Monument, started the 1890s Colorado River gold rush, became a wealthy socialite in Salt Lake City and died a hermit in Ticaboo Canyon.

The Elk Mountain Mission: A History of Moab, Mormons, The Old Spanish Trail and the Sheberetch Utes 1854 - 1855
A true story taken directly from the pioneer journals about Brigham Young's failed mission to establish a fort on the Old Spanish Trail at Moab. The mission was to help stop the New Mexican slave trade and save the souls of the Sheberetch Utes, a native tribe that would be extinct before 1880.